YOUR AGING PARENTS

YOUR AGING PARENTS

WHEN AND HOW TO HELP

Margaret J. Anderson

Publishing House
St. Louis

Copyright © 1979 by Concordia Publishing House.
Printed in the United States of America.

Library of Congress Cataloging in Publication Data

Anderson, Margaret J
    Your aging parents.

    Bibliography: p. 125
    1. Aged—Family relationships.   I. Title.
HQ1061.A575   301.42'7   78-31502
ISBN 0-570-03789-1

Acknowledgments

The author expresses gratefulness to Gilbert Moody, attorney; Donald Moline, M.D.; Howard Kanten, financial adviser; and Elizabeth Gunnear, nutritionist; for their counsel regarding areas about which they are most knowledgeable. She especially appreciates the encouragement and direction of her editor.

Contents

Introduction

This book is addressed to you who are adult children of aging parents. You may be anywhere from 40 to 65 or more years of age, with parents 60 to 90 or more years old.

As adult children you have gone through several relational cycles with your parents. After your honeymoon and the establishment of your first home you entered a withdrawal stage. Though you loved your parents, you did not want them to interfere with your life. You may have thought that you had severed the proverbial "apron strings" for good.

Then your children began to arrive. This drew your parents closer to you. They adored the grandchildren, offered to baby-sit for them and help in anyway they could. You appreciated their love and concern.

The children grew older. You climbed the economic totem pole. In time job advancements may have made it necessary for you to move great distances from your parents. Again, a time of withdrawal with attention centered on your work and your family. Distance complicated communication with your parents.

Now you find yourself in a new cycle, one in which you are concerned about your parents' future as well as the needs of your own family. Problematic as this period may be, you feel you need to be supportive of your parents, perhaps in time become their caretakers. Some call this new relationship a role-reversal stance. This concept is both inaccurate and demeaning, for you can never exchange roles with your parents. They do not become your children, nor do you become their parents. Instead you assume a new child-parent interrelational role, a filial role, which means you close the door on adolescent rebellion and early adult independence and turn to your parents with a different kind of understanding and love. You perceive them as individuals with their own rights, needs, limitations, skills, and character traits (developed long before you were born).

You put away grievances you have had against them. You forgive them. Jesus said, "If you forgive other people their failures, your Heavenly Father will also forgive you. But if you refuse to forgive other people, your Heavenly Father will not forgive you your failures" (Matt. 6:14-15 Phillips).

Forgiving is the warp, being forgiven the woof out of which the fabric of reconciliation is woven. Yet, any wrong you may need to forgive is only a tiny swatch of the bolt of debt Christ stands ready to forgive you.

A British leader, it is reported, once told John Wesley, "I never forgive."

"Then, sir," Wesley replied, "I hope that you never sin!"

All things considered, however, you feel you are caught in a bind. Some of your children may still need financial assistance. You may be facing job complications. Your wife suffers menopause difficulties. She may mourn an empty nest. Suddenly you realize you aren't as young as you used to be. You contemplate retirement and your own mortality. Torn between your family's needs and those of your parents, you wonder how well you will handle this new filial role.

Fortunately practitioners are beginning to understand and speak about your dilemma. There is literature you can read, workshops you can attend, resource persons you can consult.

This book, too, is written to assist you in resolving the problems you will face as adult children of aging parents.

1.

Old Has Many Faces

At age 65, George Keverstone, an automobile dealer, retired and turned his business over to his son's management. Then, unable to tolerate what he called a life of idleness, at 68, he went back to work on a part-time basis. At 76 he quit working for his son. He gardened, read, played golf, and assumed the financial-secretary responsibilities for his church. When he was 92, his wife died. Concerned about his welfare, his son urged him to employ a live-in couple to cook and keep house for him.

"I guess I know where the stove is," George told his son. "I doubt it will walk away. If it does, I'll eat at a restaurant. You'd think I couldn't take care of myself."

At 96, the elderly man's hearing failed to such an extent that his son bought him special earphones so he could enjoy his radio and television sets. Arthritis began to nag. Finally sensing he was slowing down, George consented to look at retirement home facilities.

In your opinion, at what point in this man's life should he be designated old?

If you were a gerontologist, you would say he was old at each of the transition points of his life. But you would qualify that statement. You would say he was *young old* at 65, *middle old* at 76, *old old* at 96.

11

Old Is Statistical

This illustration points up an interesting phenomenon regarding aging. Our concept of growing old has changed. Life expectancy has increased to such an extent that it isn't unusual to hear that a 69-year-old daughter cares for her 95-year-old mother. Families can consist not only of two or three generations, but of four and sometimes five.

Take the example of a gentleman who, when he retired at age 63, moved into the home of his daughter. He died recently, 43 years later, at age 106. The family often jokes about his longevity. "Every year," a grandson by marriage tells, "my mother-in-law urged us to make Christmas a very special occasion. It might be the last year we would have Grandfather with us. After a number of years we learned not to put much stock in her prediction."

I have been told there were five generations represented at this man's funeral. Besides the deceased, a daughter from an early marriage who was born in 1891, a younger daughter born in 1912, this woman's daughter born in 1944; and her daughter born in 1970.

Increasingly newspapers and magazines call attention to American longevity. In 1977 four centenarians, two men and two women, met in tiny Zuni Pueblo, on the western border of New Mexico. There at the Zuni tribal headquarters the governor of the state, David F. Cargo, presented them with certificates honoring their long, fruitful lives. The four: Maria Martinez, 114; Mrs. Eusalalio, 100; "Old Man Nastacio," 119; Long Kenna, 104.

Of the 4,990 inhabitants in Zuni, 96 are 80 to 119 years old. Seven are more than 100 years of age. Three of the later group did not attend the ceremony. Lorenzo, 100, was busy farming in nearby Ojo Caliente. Mrs. Ghahate, 109, a woman best known for raising luscious vegetables and fruits, especially watermelons, was baby-sitting. Mr. Yuselew, 109, the least active of the group, received his certificate of honor in his own home because he is blind.

The number of older persons in America is increasing at a faster rate than the number under 65. In the spring of 1977, the

Bureau of Census reported that there were 23 million people over 65 years of age; more than 32 million over 60. Each year one quarter million persons are added to the total over 65. Very likely there will be 30 million that age by the turn of the century when the war-baby boom shows up as a gerontological boom. Half of the population will be 50 years or older.

The Bureau of Census also indicates that life expectancy at birth for women in this country will be 81 years (it is now 76.5); for men, 71.8 (now 68.7).

Old Is Individual

What are these people like? Certainly they are not identical. They do not come in the same size, color, and shape. Nor do they carry identical labels. Neither do teenagers or infants. Older persons need to be viewed as unique persons who can still make a contribution to society, *if* society will allow them to.

Yet, we as Americans have tended to stereotype older people. Just as black Americans from the South were thought of as being lazy, dirty, and illiterate a few years ago, older Americans have too often been characterized as doddering, forgetful, poor, and unproductive.

Let's look at their individual character traits, which fall into five general classifications:[1] (1) the mature—well-integrated persons who enjoy whatever they are doing at the moment; (2) the rocking-chair type—passive, dependent men and women who are glad to take it easy; (3) the self-protective—their motto: "I have to keep active or I will die"; (4) the bitter—they adjust poorly to aging—blame others for their disappointments and lack of success; (5) the self-derogatory—depressed and gloomy, they adjust poorly, blame themselves for frustrations and failures. Each acts according to his own personality, no one else's.

Now note the desires of the elderly. They want: security—having enough funds to live a comfortable, independent life; association with other people—communication and a sense of belonging; respect for personal worth—recognition of knowledge and skills; mental stimulation—new opportunities for learning; autonomy—the right to live alone and to make their own decisions as long as they are able.[2] Invariably Christians who are elderly speak of a hope that their children will remain true to their faith.

As far as activities are concerned, older people are said to approve: accepting minor civic responsibilities; voting regularly; keeping in touch with friends and relatives by visit or mail; maintaining an active interest or hobby; being involved in the church, pursuing a social life in the community.

Old Is Variable

As you consider the elderly, you should understand that everyone doesn't age at the same rate or in the same way, no matter what his chronological age. A person may be very young yet be physically old. In my book, *Looking Ahead— The Realities of Aging: Face Them with Faith,*[3] I speak of a brilliant woman, a former drug addict now rehabilitated and active in the church and community. She looks and acts 20 years older than she is. In contrast, a healthy, energetic woman kept house for her husband and son and sang in the church choir when she was 90. She looked and acted as if she were 60.

Delayed psychological aging typifies the person who possesses a willingness to learn, a flexibility toward change, and a realistic acceptance of misfortune. One can die at 40 and be buried at 75.

Madeline Phillips' reaction to misfortune illustrates this point. Her husband died at 62. A year later, Madeline's mother, who had lived with the family for 20 years, passed away. A take-charge person, this mother had cooked, mended, and cleaned for the family. Her daughter seldom made a decision without first consulting her. Besides, Madeline had never learned to drive a car. Her husband usually did the family shopping.

Suddenly bereft of both husband and mother, Madeline crawled into an iron-coated shell of self-pity. Since she had never been required to make decisions she found she was unable to cope with life. She grew depressed. She begged God to let her die.

All forms of therapy failed. By the time she turned 60, she could be said to be psychologically old.

Older persons can also be characterized by ethnic variables. Scandinavians, for instance, are usually more reserved than Southern Europeans. Each group shows individual food preferences. To a large extent they prefer different forms of worship.

People vary, too, according to the period of history through which they lived. Mennonites who escaped from Russia carry with them prejudices which may not be as evident in the lives of their chidren born in this country. Older persons who made do or did without during the depression of the 1930s are inclined to be more frugal than their affluent children, who may earn more in one year than their parents have been able to accumulate in a lifetime.

Old Is Creative

How different from Madeline are elderly who think and act as if retirement is a period of personal growth. A friend who began writing after her children left home, produces two books a year. She is over 70. Ministers, lawyers, dentists, whoever, continue to work at self-employed activities well into their 70s or 80s.

The famous Verdi composed "Ave Maria" when he was 85. Pablo Casals played the cello, conducted orchestras, and taught music up to the time of his death at 96. Will Durant, in collaboration with his wife, Ariel, wrote five volumes of the 10-volume *History of Civilization* between 69 and 89 years of age. Konrad Adenauer remained in power in Germany until his death at 91.

Many elderly persons are following Grandma Moses' example and taking up painting. She didn't become a painter until she was 70, yet she produced more than 1,000 primitives and made herself famous before she celebrated her 100th birthday in 1961.

True, these people are exceptionally gifted individuals, yet their successes underscore the fact that creativity, industry, and willingness to serve need not dissipate with old age.

You as an adult child of aging parents may very well recognize a talent you believe a parent should develop. Voice your encouragment.

Old Is Honorable

We will all grow old if we live long enough. The elderly are persons who have lived longer than others. If your parents have health problems as they age, remember you and your children do, also.

However, older persons are much more resilient than we give them credit for. They are more self-reliant, too. Eighty-nine percent of all men and women over 65 live independently in community.

The old do not deserve useless and unproductive designations. Such terms may cause some elderly people to assume an "I'm no good—Who cares?" stance. Society's job is to encourage and esteem.

Maggie Kuhn, militant supporter of the aging, claims today's older people are a new breed of citizens. They live longer, are more vigorous physically. They are better educated, more articulate. Perceptive, they increasingly react sharply to the intolerant "put down" by society.

Older persons have a distinct advantage over those who are younger. They possess wisdom that isn't merely accumulated information. They have experienced joys, triumphs, and defeats that qualify them to advise, instruct, encourage, and console.

Consider Bernard Baruch, who advised presidents about financial matters as long as he lived. Look at San Francisco's Hasting Law School. A graduate training center for lawyers, it hires only instructors who are 65 years or older. Note also that 70 percent of all major countries in the world are headed by leaders over 60.

Mental Capacity

For too long people have erroneously believed that a person's intellectual capacity reaches its peak early in life, in the late teens or early twenties, and that from that time on it diminishes gradually. At age 65? It was thought to hit bottom.

Recent studies nix this assumption. Rule out speed, and you'll find scarcely any changes in the intellectual capacity of the elderly until very late in life. People continue to store information indefinitely. If a person knew 20,000 words when graduated from college, that number will have doubled by age 65.

Your aging parents may not recall stored information as rapidly as you, but their learning pace may equal, even exceed yours. The young, someone has said, "are quick on the trigger," the old, "slow but sure."

Older persons feel competent when they are permitted to self-pace their activities. That's why golf is a good form of recreation for these people. This may also be why writing and painting have proved so satisfying to many elderly individuals.

Commenting on capacity for learning, Dr. James E. Birren, Director of the Andrus Gerontology Center at the University of Southern California, once said, "I wouldn't feel particularly embarrassed if someone told me that I don't process as much information per unit of time as I used to. This is no ego blow to me."

He likens storing information to filing letters as they come in, chronologically; retrieving of information, to locating letters stored in that manner.

Old Is Problematic

Well adjusted as most older persons are, they do have health, housing, financial, and social problems. Were you to read their minds, you would sense the questions they ask: Should we move to a warmer climate? In what type of home should we live? Will our money last? What will happen to us if we become incapacitated? Will our children care? Will they help?

Yes, old has many faces, and God loves every one of them.

2.

Respectfully Theirs

Writing in the New York Times some years ago, James Michener described a Japanese custom that honored the elderly. On a particular occasion a red kimono presented to an elderly person made him an instant statesman and gave him the right to express his views on any subject. It also gave him the right to expect others to listen to what he had to say.

Asked by a reporter what he considered the most important asset in his country, one Japanese answered, "Our old people."

For centuries China, too, honored its elderly. Missionaries say they were considered discourteous if they failed to ask someone their senior, "How old are you?"

Two Sides of the Coin

Respect for the elderly goes back to Biblical times. The commandment to "honor your father and mother" included a promise of longevity. Other references also refer to respect for and responsibility to the elderly. Leviticus 19:32 speaks of standing in the presence of a gray-haired person to show honor and respect. Not too different from the Japanese custom of bowing when greeting older persons. Proverbs 30:17 speaks of deserved punishment for those who mock and disobey their parents. In Genesis 47:11-12 we read about Joseph demonstrating filial love when he provided for the care of his brothers and his father.

On the cross Jesus placed his mother in John's care. To John He said, "Behold your mother." To Mary, "Behold your son."

I believe there were two reasons why Jesus suggested this interpersonal accountability. Of the people gathered at Golgotha, John and Mary were apt to miss him most. By assuming a caring stance for each other, they were less apt to grovel in prolonged grief and self-pity. We infer that Joseph was dead. We do not know, however, whether John took Mary into his own home to care for her. He may have arranged for her care with someone else. Regardless, we can assume that he loved and respected her and that he kept in close contact with her.

Respect for the elderly involves a proper understanding of their problems, needs, and capabilities. Today we speak of this understanding in terms of filial maturity, which is interpersonal and involves the whole family, whether that family consists of two, three or four generations.

Yet, our nation has always placed a tremendous premium on the new and the young. We tear down the old and replace it with what we consider sophisticated and modern. And we tend to label old people as outdated and useless.

In the days of unlimited immigration, successive generations often felt they understood American life better than their parents who came from other countries. In many instances they considered parents and grandparents a source of embarrassment.

Nevertheless, older people used to live in a family situation, a closely knit social unit, especially in rural areas. They never dreamed of today's mobility. Away-from-home vacations, brief or extended, were seldom taken. Homes, as a rule, were spacious. They provided room for more than one cook as well as odd jobs for grandparents.

As their parents aged, children were expected to take care of them. Often a daughter or a bachelor son remained at home and assumed this care. Or a married son or daughter moved back to the farm to manage it when the parents were no longer able to. Sometimes the parents lived with these children. In other instances, they settled in a nearby town where their adult children could look in on them frequently.

These were the "good old days," according to some people. Yet, they may not have been as good as they are acclaimed to be. For one thing, there were fewer grandparents in that era. At the turn of the century people lived, on an average, only 48 years.

There must have been personality conflicts, tension, even bitterness at times. Having lived near my maternal grandparents when I was a child, I recall a confrontation between my mother and my grandmother, who, together with my grandfather, expected their married children to visit them on Sunday afternoons.

This particular week Mother had consented to go with Father to visit his brother's family some 30 miles away despite some special celebration at my grandparents' home.

Grandmother disapproved vigorously. It was Mother's duty . . . ! Mother must have won the argument, for we did visit Dad's brother the next weekend.

Today life is different. Relatives don't live so close together. Family homes aren't as spacious as they were. As an adult child you may have moved to the suburbs or hundreds, even thousands, of miles away from your parents.

This doesn't mean that obligations to parents have disappeared. They may have become more complicated. You respect your parents when you consider the term "senior citizen" a red kimono. Elderly people need and expect respect of younger persons. According to recent statistics, they deserve it. By holding jobs, working in church and community, participating in political procedures, organizing self-interest groups, and engaging in volunteer activities they prove this premise.

You demonstrate your respect, your filial maturity, when you keep communication lines open. When you listen. I often hear adults whose parents have died say, "Why didn't we ask them about their youth?" This, too, is my regret.

I wish I had asked for details about the scary winter trips my father took over a chain of lakes in northern Minnesota when he was young. The purpose: to bring supplies by horse and sled from Winnipeg to the Iron Range where he lived. What a wonderful book-length juvenile story that would make.

You demonstrate respect when you honor parents' feelings and desires. Several years ago a *Woman's Day* story[1] portrayed the other side of honor's coin. It told of a nursing home resident's determination to go to the polls and vote as he had always done. No one respected his wish. The director and one staff member in particular scoffed at the idea. The man's daughter, who had promised to pick him up, phoned late that morning to tell him she wouldn't be able to make it. Her excuse was trivial.

Involve Grandchildren

You demonstrate parental respect when you teach your children to honor their grandparents. You do this chiefly by example. My husband wrote his father once a week while he was living. Now our son writes to us once a week. I am confident his children will write their parents when they leave home.

At a recent conference a gerontologist spoke of sending his daughter, restless and indifferent about her future, to visit his parents one summer. The girl became so enamored by her grandparents she decided to interview them and write biographies about them. In doing so, she learned new appreciation for them, for her father, and for herself.

Says her father, "She knows more about our roots than any other member of the family. More important, she has learned older people have something important to say."

Margaret Mead frequently asked her students to interview older people. At one time they developed a model book, *How to Interview Your Grandfather.* The students formulated their interview questions simply by pondering the things they wanted to know about the past. You may not be a teacher, nevertheless, you can encourage your children to write about your parents.

It is equally important to encourage your parents to write about themselves. A 1979 Herald Press release, *Good Times with Old Times,* written by Katie Funk Wiebe, not only nudges older persons to write their own stories but gives explicit instruction how to do so. Designated memoirs rather than biographies, these stories are important because they establish continuity with the past that will enable you and your children to live more satisfactorily and fully in the future.

Whatever the interaction with the elderly, they appreciate whatever attention they receive.

One cold winter day a clergyman and his wife visited an elderly couple. The occasion: the woman's 80th birthday.

"It's our son's birthday today, too," the pastor's wife informed the woman.

"It is? I remember him well. He greeted my husband and me briefly as he passed us in the church foyer one Sunday. Then he stopped, turned, and came back to speak to us. I don't remember what we talked about. But I can tell you it was a pleasure to have a younger person take notice."

Perhaps there are things you can do to convince the young people in your family and church that older people enjoy talking to them.

Attitude of Professionals

Someone has said many individuals are more comfortable with the blind, deaf, or handicapped than with the elderly. These people fail to realize that most older persons read newspapers, magazines, and books. Many are creative, understanding, and tolerant. They continue to be interested in local, state, and federal affairs.

Recently a 65-year-old son called his 96-year-old Illinois mother from California.

"Do you know what, Dow?" his mother began. "The local newspaper is going to run a feature article about me. They sent a reporter to interview me."

"Be sure you send me a copy," Dow told his mother.

"Oh, I don't know about that. It will be just like all other articles about old people. They didn't ask me a single important question." She paused for a moment, then, "Say, Dow, how do you feel about the Panama Treaty?"

Even doctors tend to demean the elderly. In his book, *Why Survive? Being Old in America,*[2] Dr. Robert N. Butler tells a story about a Sam Morris who consulted his doctor about a pain in his left leg.

Seeking to distract the older man, the doctor said, "Sam, for Peter's sake, what do you expect at 102?"

Sam's retort: "Look, my right leg is 102 years old, too. But it doesn't hurt. How do you explain that?"

Evidence of Social Concern

I'm not discouraged by such an incident, common as it may be. Society, so long concerned about infancy, youth, and middle age has begun to focus its attention on old age. Now we hear references to words derived from the Greek *geron* (old man): gerontology, geopsychiatry, geriatrics.

The White House Conference on Aging, the passage of the Older American Act, and the creation of the Administration on Aging under the Department of Health, Education, and Welfare, indicates efforts are being made to improve the lot of older Americans. Note, too, the concern of such organizations as the Gray Panthers, the Congress for Senior Citizens and the American Association of Retired Persons.

Older people are saying:

> Look at me,
> Please, look at me;
> Where I am
> You someday will be.

Increasingly there are those who are looking. They are listening, too.

3.

Consider Feelings

Most adult children agree that aging parents deserve respect and supportive concern. The degree to which this respect and concern is demonstrated, however, depends to a large extent on feelings—feelings about parents and feelings between siblings.

We should be aware that it's possible to experience a wide range of emotions. Some of them, if unresolved, may hinder rather than help solve an older person's problems.

Carry-over Feelings

Most frequently our emotions evolve from experiences we had as children. If you never saw people reach out to help others, you would find it difficult to express yourself in that manner. On the other hand, if your parents were warm and compassionate, no doubt you are, too.

Children who have never known love and tenderness may, as they grow older, find it difficult to be warm and tender toward their aging parents. Recently a woman in her 70s spoke to me about her 90-year-old mother whom she visits in a nursing home several times a month. "I have to admit," she said, "that I have no warm feelings toward my mother."

"But why?" I asked. "You are a warm person. You're always going out of your way for others."

"If I have any warmth, it came from my grandmother.

When my mother remarried following the death of my father, she placed me, the baby of the family, in my grandmother's care. Her new husband didn't want me. So, you see, it was Grandmother who taught me what love means. I used to feel bitter. I don't anymore. I just feel sorry for my mother."

This experience illustrates the fact that feelings we have about our parents may be those we have always had. We may have pushed them into our subconscious only to have them emerge later in confrontations with our parents. Yet, as was the case with this woman, once we admit and accept these feelings and place them in their proper perspective, we are freed to behave more effectively.

Mistakes we attribute to our parents in our growing-up years may still rankle. Yet, we are apt to perceive them differently now. "My dad could easily have been a twin brother to Scrooge," may be replaced by, "I wonder how he managed to raise six kids on that barren farm in northern Minnesota." "I thought my parents unbearably strict when I was young. Now when I see the excessive permissiveness of some parents, I'm glad mine kept a tight rein on me."

Composite Feelings

You may find that love, respect, compassion and concern can exist simultaneously in your relationship with your aging parents. Or you may find that one emotion predominates or contradicts another. A son may respect his traveling-salesman father yet feel he has never been close to him, has never learned to love him. Instead he carries resentments that grew out of his father's frequent absences from home. However, he may, at this point, feel responsible for his father's care.

Conversely, a woman's lack of love may spring from a lifetime of overindulgence on the part of her parents. Now when it's her turn to be concerned about their welfare, she may feel selfishly resentful because they are dependent and can no longer do for her. She may find it difficult to reach out to them.

Further, children may respect their parents yet dislike what they call "narrow-minded" attitudes. These children, someone has said, find it easier to love at a distance.

Fear, Anxiety, Hostility

Adult children may feel fear or anxiety as their parents age. They may fear: sibling misunderstanding; their parents' disapproval; long-term health care; their impending death; the loss of an inheritance. Or they may feel worried because they have never been able to live up to their parents' expectations.

Anger and hostility, even contempt, may surface when an adult child recalls tragedies he experienced in his or her youth.

I have three friends, a ventriloquist evangelist, a woman writer, and a food-supplement salesman, whose fathers walked out on them when they were small children. In most instances, the children felt disappointment and anger. The older children, in particular, could not forget that they had to forfeit college educations while helping support their families.

Reunions (in each case the prodigal father returned years later) were complicated by a complexity of emotions.

Yet it is in just such instances that Christianity unfurls its white banner of truce. The father of the ventriloquist evangelist, Joy Cummings, made his whereabouts known shortly after Joy's mother passed away. The family asked Joy to visit him. "Because bitterness still rankled, I felt I couldn't face him," Joy told me. "Then I remembered how fervently our mother had prayed for him through the years. I consented to visit him."

"I broke down when he asked me to forgive him. We made our peace, and then, after I told him about my mother's prayers, he committed his life to Jesus Christ."

My author friend's mother had also passed away when her father contacted the family. Having become a Christian, he asked to be reunited with and forgiven by the family. My friend visited him as soon as possible. When he died, several members of the family flew across the country to attend his funeral.

When my salesman friend was 12 years old, his father deserted his mother and five children for another woman. His mother died shortly afterward. Twenty years ago the father, who had remarried, contacted the family.

When he and his wife aged to the extent they could no longer live alone, my friend built an addition to his home and cared for them until their death.

"I can't say I ever respected or loved my father, but I forgave him and built a relationship of a sort with him," the son tells. "I guess I still mourn the loss of years when we might have been close."

Shame

Many people feel shame at some point in life. For some adult children shame can be a constant companion. They may experience shame because they haven't accomplished what their parents have. Perhaps in time of need their parents contributed money toward their support. Now unable to repay, they feel ashamed.

As has been suggested previously, there are adult children who feel shame because their parents are poor or uneducated or because they are not as sophisticated as they should be. Parents who are alcoholics cause shame. A son may discover his mother is a kleptomaniac. He is ashamed as well as fearful someone may learn of her actions. Then, to further complicate matters, adult children may feel ashamed of being ashamed.

Guilt

This leads directly to another feeling—guilt. The daughter who is ashamed of her parents feels guilty because she does. Rarely does one emotion stand alone. Guilt, however, seems the most difficult feeling to handle.

What is guilt? It is a feeling of responsibility for offenses; remorse for doing wrong. Horace Bushnell said, "Guilt is the very nerve of sorrow."

Shakespeare: "The mind of guilt is full of scorpions." Further, ". . . they whose guilt within their bosom lies, imagine every eye beholds their blame."

Authors Barbara Silverstone and Helen Kandel Hyman define guilt as "hidden or exposed emotion that alerts us to our own sense of wrong-doing in words or deeds or even thoughts. It is often accompanied by lowered self-esteem and a wish to be punished.

"In present-day thinking, guilt feelings are often attributed to personal neurosis or wishes not rooted in the real world around us. But guilt is not always buried. It should be remembered that people can also feel very guilty for things they have actually done or not done—for sins of commission as well as omission. In that respect guilt means accepting responsibility for actions taken or evaded, and within reasonable limits can be a sign of emotional maturity."[1]

These women also say that the more guilt we feel the more difficult it is for us to behave responsibly. Responsible behavior comes more easily when we understand not only our parents but ourselves and our feelings toward them.

A son may say, "My mother took care of my grandmother and my dad when they became terminally ill. Now she has had a stroke. Yet, it is impossible for me to take her into my home and care for her. I must be satisfied that she is comfortable and well fed in a nursing home." This type of reasoning represents a responsible approach, not a guilty one.

Parent-induced Guilt

Sometimes parents place guilt upon their children. "Don't mind me," they say. "Keep your appointment. I'm used to staying alone." Or, "Think of all we did for you when you were a child. How can you move so far from us now?"

A 45-year-old daughter, who had remained at home and cared for her parents, met and fell in love with a widower in a nearby town. She promised to marry him.

Her parents were incensed. "Leave us? After all the years we have taken care of you!"

Greatly perturbed, the daughter sought counsel of her pastor. After he had helped her resolve her guilt, the girl went ahead with her plans.

In a similar instance, it was a sister who doled out the guilt. After being graduated from college and accepting good jobs, Dola and Mildred continued to live with their parents. When Dola, 39, told her sister, 42, that she planned to marry a man she loved very much, Mildred accused her of disloyalty. "You can't leave the folks now. They are going to need us more than ever in the years to come."

Fortunately Dola didn't feel guilty about her action. She felt she had done no wrong in God's sight. Consequently she married in spite of her sister's protestations.

A discussion of guilt would not be complete without a reference to the guilt sons and daughters feel when they wish, even pray, that their aging mother or father would die. A son may say, "I hope Dad can die soon. I can't stand to see him suffer much longer."

This it seems is a wish that society understands and condones. A less acceptable desire and one perhaps more guilt inducing, involves a difficult, incapacitated parent whose care has sapped the strength of the son or daughter responsible for the long period at caring. The attending adult may say, "I wish my mother (or father) would die. I don't believe I can hold out.

Deserved Guilt

Admittedly, some children deserve the accusation, "They don't care one hoot what happens to their aging parents." Such persons, who may live around the block or hundreds of miles away, have turned their back on their parents. An anniversary or birthday card, an occasional phone call, or a monthly check soothes their conscience.

This kind of guilt, however, can cause children to behave inappropriately toward their parents. Realizing they fall short, they may become overly protective. Or they may withdraw completely from further responsibility, saying, "Let Harry take care of the folks. He was always their favorite."

A guilty person may also become vindictive, even punitive in his treatment of aging parents. In such an instance it may be necessary for others to intervene.

The Guilt Everyone Shares

Most adult children feel guilty because they can never do for their parents what they did for them. Often following their demise, other guilty feelings surface: "We didn't write or phone often enough when they were living." Or, "We weren't able to care for them in our own homes."

I recall the time I was asked to sign papers that would

commit my senile mother to institutional care.

At the time I was in a hospital following back surgery made necessary because of a ruptured disc incurred when I cared for her.

I picked up a pen, but I could not force myself to add my name to the list of siblings who had already signed the document. I wept bitterly. When my surgeon entered the room he asked me what was wrong. I told him.

I'll never forget his counsel. It helped alleviate the guilt I felt. "If your mother suffered from some other illness with which you were unable to cope, you'd place her where she could get the best care possible, wouldn't you?"

It's well to acknowledge guilt, but it's more important that it be examined and resolved. Many times the guilt we feel is inaccurately appropriated. Filial maturity requires that we examine our feelings for what they are—most often, natural reactions to the problems we face.

When you say, "I feel guilty, I don't know what to do about my mother (or my father)," you may feel overwhelmed by the problems with which you must cope. Practitioners advise separating your problems into manageable segments and handling them, at your convenience, one at a time.

Sadness and regret may also masquerade as guilt. You may feel badly because your mother has to suffer, or you may regret that you can't do more, but you needn't interpret these emotions as guilt.

Always be sure you differentiate between true guilt and false guilt. If an action can be categorized as wrong in the sight of God according to Biblical teachings, if you know God would not approve, you can be quite sure you experience true guilt. If, on the other hand, after prayer and consultation with professionals, you did the best you know how and you are aware of no wrongdoing for which God would hold you accountable, you may assume the guilt you feel is false.

But do remember, if you feel guilt is deserved, you don't have to grovel in it. We have a compassionate God who *understands* and *forgives* whether the infraction involving our aging parents be one of omission or commission.

4.

Who Is
Your Parents' Keeper?

Emma Warda, a widow, 80 years old, lives alone in a house to the east of the one my husband and I own. Helen Lindahl, 86, also a widow, lives alone in the house to the west of us.

Emma, an Austrian, takes daily walks, visits her hairdresser weekly and carefully watches her diet so she won't gain weight. Her daughter and son-in-law, who live in a city 20 miles away, visit her once a week. They make sure that mother's larder is stocked and that her lawn is mowed and bushes and shrubs tended.

Who is Emma's keeper? Not her daughter and son-in-law. Emma is.

Helen, a Scandinavian, has a bad heart. She has been in the hospital two times in the last two years. Yet, she manages to maintain her home and cook for herself. She hires a man to care for her lawn. Her son and daughter-in-law, who live 80 miles away, visit her once or twice a month.

Who is Helen's keeper? Not her son and daughter-in-law. Helen is.

When I speak of the independence of these two women, I do not in any way minimize their adult children's love, concern, and counsel. I designate their role as *supportive*, not *custodial* caretaking.

Emma and Helen represent a large segment, 80 percent, of the independent elderly who live in their own homes. They belong to a group, four fifths of the noninstitutionalized, who have living children. Their children represent one fourth of the adults in the United States who have at least one living parent.

As adult children of aging parents you, too, may be providing supportive love and concern. The time may come, just as it may come for Emma's and Helen's children, when that role changes and you actually become your parents' caretakers.

It surprised me to learn that 20 million persons over 65 have no families to care for them. Yet, millions of other elderly people are not so alone. And, despite the assumption that children grow up and move away, studies reveal that 85 percent of the elderly have at least one child who lives less than an hour away and that 66 percent saw one of their children the very day they were interviewed. Only 2 percent had not seen their children during the past year.[1]

Millions of adult children, regardless of geographical location, are concerned about their aging parents. In times of serious crisis, sons and daughters usually carry responsibilities involved. But others, friends and neighbors and other relatives, may offer help, give suggestions, advice, and as one woman put it, criticism.

Usually everyone benefits from this united concern whether it involves a need that requires only supportive assistance or represents a crisis situation. In either instance family members who respond may find they are drawn closer together. Hurts that have smoldered for years may evaporate in the warmth of mutual concern. Yet, what may evoke unity and closeness in one family may spark a civil war in another. The reason: families are made up of varied personalities, temperaments, and capabilities. In some instances these traits fuse beautifully, in others they cause such cleavage that outside counsel may be required.

The handling of responsibilities can be affected by the

position different members hold in the family structure. Sometimes the oldest child has been the most involved with aging parents. On the other hand, this individual could have married first and in the ensuing separation left parents in a younger sibling's care.

Certainly this was true in days past. My husband's aunt, one of his mother's younger sisters, lived with and cared for both grandparents as long as they lived. However, his sister, because she lived next door, assumed the supportive care of their parents when they became ill—a caretaker role for their mother after their father passed away.

Someone, it seems, regardless of age or proximity, needs to be chosen or to volunteer to "look after parental needs." Not alone, however. The rest of the family ought to do their part. If a parent is barely able to exist on a small pension and/or Social Security check, one or more of the children may choose to supplement that income.

Sensible?

Before you answer, contemplate the questions practitioners ask about these contributions: Is the money provided out of generosity or out of a sense of guilt? Are any strings attached ("If I give so much, I should be entitled to this or that heirloom, or the bank stocks, whatever, when Mom dies.")? Will parents be required to account for every penny they spend?

Further: Does the monthly check compare favorably with the personal assistance, weekly visits, grocery shopping trips, periodic housecleaning tasks of other siblings?

We might ask, in any type of supportive care, how husbands and wives resolve difficulties that might arise. Is there ever friction? Yes, in some instances. A husband may love his mother-in-law, yet be extremely jealous of the time his wife spends with her. As likely, a husband may be very supportive of his wife in her concern for her parents. Problems escalate more often when the care of the parents disrupts and harms the caring person's family.

Grandchildren, too, need to be involved in a family's concern for grandparents. How much they become involved, however, depends largely on you, their parents. How you feel and behave toward your parents can affect your children's feelings and behavior toward them.

Studies have confirmed that there is a great deal of rapport between grandchildren and grandparents. When grandparents grow old, grandchildren often assist in any way they can.

I recall with deep gratitude the love and concern our daughter, Laurine, then a high school student, showed my mother during the period of time she lived with us prior to my back surgery. Because Mother suffered severe brain damage from arteriosclerosis, she didn't always stay in bed when she retired. She'd get up and dress, assuming she had slept for some time. Repeatedly, and with great patience, Laurine persuaded her to undress and go back to bed.

In a supportive role you will be alert to your parent's needs. You will stand by, listen, and give advice when asked. When your parents can no longer live alone, you may be required to assume a caretaker role. Then you will shoulder responsibilities they can no longer handle.

In both the supportive and caretaker roles, you will walk a tight rope. You'll be wise to accept the counsel of people who say, "Do what is comfortable and acceptable to your parents as long as you anticipate no serious repercussions in allowing them to determine what actions should be taken."

If, instead of demanding that your parents follow your suggestions, you are able to show concern, patience, and understanding, given time, they'll probably work out their own solutions in their own way. The danger is that too often adult children talk around their parents. They make decisions without consulting them. Nothing is more demeaning and unkind.

You are also advised not to be overly protective of the elderly. If your father insists he is able to mow the lawn, let him. If your mother continues gardening long after you think she should desist, for fear she will fall and break a limb, don't interfere. She can also fall in her bedroom or in the kitchen.

Two sons of an aging physician asked a friend, a family counselor, what they should do about their father's driving.

"Is he a good driver? Likely to harm anyone?" the man asked.

"No, we don't think so. It's just that he is getting terribly forgetful. Often he forgets to turn off the freeway at the right exit."

"So? What harm if he drives a few extra miles?"

Finally, remember that how you behave toward your parents may be reflected later in the behavior of your children toward you. A Pakistani folktale (varied versions are found in other cultures) makes this point extremely well.

An aged grandmother lived with her daughter and grandson in a small house at the edge of a village.

As the grandmother aged, she grew frail and feeble, and her eyesight deteriorated. She forgot where she had placed things. She broke plates and cups and made herself a nuisance when her daughter cooked for the family.

One day, provoked because her mother had broken another cherished plate, the daughter gave her son some money and told him to go to the village for her. "Buy Grandmother a wooden plate," she said. "She won't be able to break that."

The boy hesitated. He had learned that wooden plates were meant only for peasants and servants, not for a good woman like his grandmother.

However, after some insistance on the part of his mother, he did as he was told. In time he returned with not one, but two wooden plates.

Provoked, the mother asked, "Didn't I say one? Why did you buy two?"

"Because . . . ," the boy stammered. "I . . . I thought I ought to buy a second one so I'd have one for you when you grow old."

5.

Living Options

Given a choice, most older persons indicate they wish to remain in their own homes as long as they can. And most often they can, if they maintain good health. When one spouse dies, other arrangements may be considered. Yet this need not be the case, as noted in the previous chapter when Emma and Helen were introduced.

There are advantages in remaining in the "home place." Most likely it is paid for; if not, it carries a low-interest, long-term mortgage loan. Owners continue to enjoy the fellowship of long-time friends. Nearby shops, parks, banks, and churches wear familiar, comfortable labels.

However, we acknowledge the fact that we live in a mobile society, where the elderly are as apt to get itchy feet as the young. Move or stay, it is of prime importance that they be allowed to maintain an independent life-style.

Should Your Parents Move?

If and when your parents begin to wonder whether or not they should move, you may be the one to whom they turn for advice. If their home is too large, the yard unmanageable, your parents may sell their residence and rent an apartment or buy a mobile home. Whichever, they will want to compare current expenses—taxes, insurance, and upkeep—with apartment rents and mobile-home space assessments.

On the other hand, they could convert their home into two apartments and rent one of them. Individuals can be hired for cleaning and yard work.

Suppose, however, that health or the desire to live near you or one of the other children, prompts them to relocate. Before you make any suggestions you may wish to consider the following questions: Are they the type of people who adjust to change easily? Will a warm climate or nearness to children (who may be transferred within a year or two) offset separation from old friends, other relatives, warm church and community ties?

Recently a visitor expressed concern for an elderly mother who lives in a suburb of North London.

"She visited with our family the past month," he said. "Last Saturday I put her on a return plane. Try as my brother and I did, we couldn't persuade her to move to this country so we could more easily look after her. I can understand why. It would be extremely difficult to leave the old haunts."

I know of no statistics that determine the number of people who have retraced their steps after making a move they believed would be permanent. It may be formidable. My husband and I just received word that friends who had moved to Mesa, Arizona, seven years ago, had sold their lovely mobile home and returned to Denver, Colorado. Reason? They missed their friends and family.

No doubt more elderly persons adjust to new environments than those who do not. Chiefly, I believe, because they planned their move and chose their retirement home with great care. This planning should involve visiting, perhaps even living, in the area or facility for a time on a trial basis. It would also involve investigating churches, banks, and availability of good medical care. Cost must also be appraised.

Suppose a parent is a widow who suffers from arthritis. Her doctor suggests a warm climate. Her problem: money. She lives on a small pension and Social Security check. Her husband's terminal illness cut a huge swatch out of their meager savings. Were she your parent, what would you recommend she do?

Government-Subsidized Housing

You might advise she investigate government-subsidized housing. Public housing, which used to serve only low income families with children, has been extended to include older persons. Available in most areas, this housing ranges from attached one-story buildings to high-rise structures. Both types provide comfortable studio or one-bedroom apartments for persons with low incomes. They provide safety equipment, laundry rooms, and recreational facilities. Ability to pay determines rental prices.

Life-Care Facilities

Increasingly life-care facilities are chosen by elderly persons who wish to exchange home chores and worries for more leisurely living. Life-care is usually a non-profit arrangement made available by philanthropic, fraternal, and religious organizations. Facilities range from luxurious high-rise apartments to pleasant studio, one-bedroom or two-bedroom apartments arranged dormitory fashion. Some facilities also have duplexes or small cottages which are separate from the main buildings. Life-care promises retired persons a place to live, nutritious meals, medical attention, and recreational facilities as long as they live.

Entrance requires residents pay a founder's or development fee that is not refundable after a specific period of time. Monthly charges range from $250 to $400, or even $600 a month depending on distinctiveness of the facility. Each unit usually contains a central lounge, a dining room, recreational, shop and craft centers, a library, laundry room, and accomodations for entertainment of private guests.

A great deal of apprehension was created about life-care centers when the "60-Minute" television program presented sordid details of a facility that went bankrupt and left its residents without a place to live.

This particular example is one of only a few such cases

among the 900 residential care and life-care communities that serve as home for some 240,000 retired people. Any facility, if not managed properly, can fail. Thus it behooves you to be concerned about the financial stability of any retirement center your parents consider. Ask for, and have a lawyer check, the facility's audited financial statements. Investigate the reputation of developers. Study contracts to determine monthly fees, allowances for price change, rules regarding decoration of apartments, and visitor privileges. Look for hidden costs, charges for "extra favors." Determine what training and experience the administrator has had.

My denomination, the Evangelical Covenant Church of America, operates 16 life-care centers. Increasingly administrators are persons with education and experience that qualify them for their job. Covenant Village, located in the city where I live, was built adjacent to our denomination's health care center and nursing home. Across the street is a modern, well-equipped hospital that doctors claim is far superior to those in cities of a comparable population.

A couple who moved into the center when it opened had lived in a Florida mobile home for several years following the husband's retirement. They say, "We enjoy having our meals prepared for us. We enjoy the fellowship of other residents and the facilities the center provides. But, more important, we are at ease knowing our children won't be burdened with our care when we become ill or incapacitated."

Other church groups are also involved in life-care community services. Write your denomination for a list of addresses.

Other Residential Facilities

In many areas comfortable privately owned residential hotels cater to retired persons. Operated as profit-making business ventures, they provide rooms and apartments with utilities, maid service, and recreational facilities included in the rental fee. In some instances meals are included, in others they can be purchased in the hotel's cafeteria/dining room. Owners will arrange medical care if residents desire.

Church, philanthropic, and fraternal organizations provide apartments or small-cottage rental housing for self-sufficient persons who cherish their independence. Utilities as well as recreational facilities are included in the rental fee. Most of these rentals maintain a special arrangement with doctors and hospitals. A charge may be made for such service, or its cost may be included in the monthly rental fee.

You should be aware, too, of the retirement villages that appeal to older persons. Such villages are a community of houses and apartments that resemble a small city, except that residents must be over 50 or 55 years of age. Villages, for the most part, are self-governing. Sun City, a retirement community near Phoenix, Arizona, with its churches, banks, hospital, doctors' building, golf course, recreational buildings, and restaurants, has grown so rapidly it resembles a large city.

For a comprehensive list of retirement-facility addresses write to the Retirement Research and Welfare Association, 215 Long Beach Blvd., Long Beach, California. You will be sent free listings in any three states you specify.

The Live-with-Children Option

A consideration of retirement-living options would not be complete without a reference to the arrangement where elderly parents (or parent) live with one of their children. Speaking of this arrangement to a friend one day, I said, "I wouldn't want to live with my children."

My friend countered, "Don't say that. God may have some purpose in such an arrangement. You may have lessons to learn. Conversely, there are many things your grandchildren and children may learn from you."

I had never thought of three-generation living in this light. I do recall, however, adults who, in relating stories about live-in grandparents, expressed great satisfaction with the arrangement. One woman said, "Grandmother had a decisive influence on my life. When I came home from school I went directly to her room. She read to me, told me stories about her past, and helped me with my schoolwork."

When I think of the short time my mother lived in our

home I am aware that, in helping care for her, my daughter learned patience, love, and respect for elderly people.

Howard Whitman, who has written widely about human relations, asks, "Why shouldn't aging parents, if they have done their job raising their children and shouldered the burden of their education, be able to accept warmly and graciously a helping hand from those for whom they toiled?" [1]

I suppose no one can determine which families would profit by having an elderly parent live with them or which would be worse off. A recent television film, "A Family Upside Down," featuring Helen Hays and Fred Astaire, revealed how one very loving family was torn between loyalties, devotion, frustration of a teenager, and parental guilt. [2] In an article, "I Had to Ask My Mother to Move Out of My House," [3] one woman told how, unable to cope with attendant frustrations, she found an apartment for her mother in a retirement facility. The mother blossomed, took a new interest in life, learned to enjoy her surrogate family to such an extent that broken family relationships were healed and became respectful and congenial again.

If you feel strongly that you should invite a parent, a mother perhaps, to live with you, yet are reluctant, realize you are not alone. National surveys reveal both elderly parents and their children feel this same reluctance.

Some children decide to share the responsibility of housing a parent. Mother may live with a daughter during the summer months, with a son during the winter. Or a parent may spend three or four months with each.

I have always thought this is a questionable arrangement for parents. Living out of suitcases, they exist in constant change with no place they really can call home.

Your own mother may be the type who prefers not living with you. Or she may be one who pleads with you to take her in. In either case, though you hesitate, you may feel it is your duty to make a home for her.

Whatever your decision, it should not be made hastily or sentimentally, or be based on what other people think, but on a rational analysis of your family's situation. Ask God's guidance as you weigh the following questions:

Is your spouse agreed that having your mother in your home is wise? What about financial arrangement? Does your home provide ample room for everyone? Cramped living can be devastating to everyone. Do you honestly believe you can live together comfortably in peace? Will your mother forego interfering with the running of the household or the rearing of the children? Is her temperament, education, and social experience such that she will fit into your family and be comfortable with your friends? Will her constant presence rob you of the privacy you cherish?

If after weighing these questions you say, "it would never work," make other arrangements. It is easier to do so now than later.

On the other hand, you may say, "There may be minor problems, but we can work them out. We always have in the past. Mother isn't a buttinsky. She and my wife get along famously." Then you may wish to ask your mother to live with you.

Many people believe three-generation living works best when the elderly parents' living quarters are separate yet a part of the family home. Then grandparents can rest, read, retire when they wish. They can listen to their choice of radio or television programs at whatever volume they select. Yet, they are free to join the family and help if they desire.

As in any arrangement, there are pitfalls and advantages. Note the pitfalls that are apt to present problems:

* Differences in amusements, manners, and values can cause friction.

* Grandparents may overindulge the grandchildren or take sides with them against their parents.

* The elderly may compete with parents for the children's affection.

* Grandparents occasionally advise and direct when they shouldn't.

Now, note the advantages:

* Older persons may widen their grandchildren's horizons.

* They can bolster their faith; lead them to a personal commitment to Christ.

* They can teach children skills parents do not have time for.

* Grandparents supply extra hands when work schedules overwhelm their children.

* Grandparents give grandchildren a sense of continuity; of heritage.

Assessing this list, we might say, "Pitfalls, once recognized, can be avoided; advantages, once discovered, can be enjoyed."

Moving Assistance

When the time comes for your parents to make a move, whether it be to your home, to a retirement village, a life-time care facility, a mobile home, or an apartment, they may have little use for a great many of their possessions. You can help them dispose of what they don't need.

A warning: urge them to start early and take their time. That was the intention of a Midwestern friend. Having paid her entrance fee for an apartment in an under-construction life-care facility, she knew she would have to dispose of a great many pieces of furniture, books, kitchenware, dishes, nick-nacks, and odds and end. Since the administrator of the facility agreed she could take possession of her apartment as much as two months after opening date, she felt relieved because she would not need to hurry.

She began by setting aside items her children wanted. Then she advertised and sold furniture items she couldn't use, retaining to sell later the pieces that would enhance the sale of the house. In time she'd advertise a garage sale.

The retirement facility opened. My friend wasn't worried, she had plenty of time. Then, suddenly, plenty-of-time disappeared like a puff of wind. A daughter who lived in St. Louis, Missouri, phoned. "Mom, Sis and I are flying in on Wednesday. We'll help you pack and get you settled in your apartment. But first we'll help you with your garage sale."

"But I'm not ready!"

"You'll have to be. This is the only time we can come."

You can imagine the panic my friend experienced.

After she had moved into her apartment she found she had sold articles she wanted to keep and kept articles for which she had no need.

How different the experience of a local resident. Her children advised her not to part with a thing until she had settled into the life-care facility she had chosen. In that way, she could determine exactly what she needed and wanted to keep. After they had helped their mother move, her children took charge of a "moving sale" at the home place.

Ingenious? Indeed.

If a parent or parents live a great distance from their future home, it may be more difficult to know what to discard and sell and what to keep. Experienced individuals advise older people, "When in doubt, take questionable items with you. It's better to be safe than sorry. You can always dispose of excess baggage at your new location."

6.
Quality of Life

* A school principal dictates his last letter, an application for his retirement pension.
* A business executive hands his office keys to an eager colleague who trails him on the organization's totem pole.
* A gray-haired librarian stamps her last "date due" in an avid reader's armload of books.
* A retired minister packs his briefcase and heads for home.

　　To what?

　　To long neglected household chores; to a continual round of golf; to some southern clime; to baby-sitting; a good book and a comfortable rocking chair.

Thus began an article I wrote a few years ago about the potential of the elderly. I added:

But eventually household chores are completed, golf, gluttony, baby-sitting, and rocking chairs lose their initial appeal. Soon a nostalgic longing for challenging communication, involvement, and recognition of personal worth nags the soul.

What did I refer to?

A *quality of life* for the elderly. A chief concern for many as is evidenced by comments such as: "Don't rig up childish entertainment for us." "These kiddy songs and charity programs are an insult to what intelligence we have left." "I want to communicate, to be a part of the stream of life." "Life must continue being meaningful."

Communication

In recent years practitioners, concerned about parent and teenager relationships, have constantly advised: "Keep the lines of communication open." This advice is just as apt when we speak of filial (age-inclusive) relationships with special emphasis on communication between adult children and their elderly parents.

To be old often means to be shut out. Among the most lonely people are those who feel isolated from life. It's difficult to perceive the isolation felt by the 50 percent of the elderly who have no children. Harder to perceive why those who have children ever need to feel isolated.

On one visit to Los Angeles my husband and I looked up a woman who, suffering from multiple sclerosis, lived in a nursing home facility. We found her huddled in a wheel chair, shivering in a threadbare sweater in the afternoon cool of the day. Immobile, but clear of mind, she greeted us, "Thank you, thank you for coming. I don't have many visitors anymore."

If you wish to add quality to your parents' lives, "Keep the lines of communication open."

Visit them as often as you can. Recently I spoke to a woman who hadn't had a visit from her son's family for 10 years. "I don't know my own grandchildren," she said.

If your parents are in good health, send the grandchildren for a visit.

Telephone. Let your parents know you are thinking about them even if they are a continent away. Several long distance phone calls cost a fraction of a trip of hundreds of miles.

If you live near, get involved in some of their interests. Spend an evening playing games, bowling, whatever; an afternoon playing golf. Fashion your mother's hair. Do errands that are difficult for your parents to do.

And permit them to do things for you. Let them take your family to dinner if they can afford to. Show interest in their advice even if you ignore it. Discuss problems with them. Hug them and tell them you love them.

Remember birthdays and anniversaries with an ingeniously selected card or gift.

It isn't easy to buy gifts for the elderly. Yet a little creativity on your part may surprise you. Recently I queried specifically selected elderly parents, asking them what gifts they would prefer not to receive at the present time. Note the responses:

"No ties or cologne."

"Shirts? My closets are full of them!"

"I don't need any more nighties or negligees."

"Perfume? I have enough to last me a lifetime."

What then?

The following list names gifts these same people said they had enjoyed receiving:

A humming-bird feeder

Oil paints and brushes

Two dozen tulip bulbs

A smoke alarm

A kitchen stool

"Reach-for" tongs

A sweater

Stamps and stationery

Gift certificates

Large print books and magazine subscriptions

National Geographic subscription

A subscription for a favorite religious periodical

Airplane tickets to a restful retreat

Up-to-date picture of the grandchildren

An airplane ticket to visit the family

Books (One woman indicated she always sends her children a list to choose from.)

No doubt you can add a great many gifts ideas if you zero in on the interests, needs, and pleasures of your parents.

Gifts chosen for nursing home residents are more difficult to select. A woman who had subscribed to *Better Homes and Gardens* for her mother wondered why old copies lay unread in a pile beside her bed.

A friend suggested, "Those magazines are for active women who have homes and kitchens. Your mother has neither. Besides the magazine may be too awkward for her to hold, the print too small." The daughter immediately subscribed for the mini-sized *Have a Happy Day* periodical for her mother.

A wise woman brought her mother a rose in a small bud vase. The vase robbed little of the scanty space on her bedside table. And it could be replenished periodically.

Because these people cannot shop for themselves, they appreciate writing paper, envelopes, postage stamps, and toilet articles they use frequently. They also enjoy an occasional automobile ride; a visit when you read the Bible or some other book to them; candy (if permitted) and fruit.

Involvement

Quality of life isn't measured only by communication and gifts, however. Your parents want to be involved in activities they can handle comfortably.

They may wish to continue their education. "Life-time learning" is a new option for the elderly. Individuals in their 70s and 80s now complete work for specific degrees under this program.

If you are interested in discovering your "roots," ask your parents to write their biographies for you. A meaningful experiment in biography writing by elderly persons has been conducted by the Andrus Gerontology Center, Los Angeles, with remarkable results. The elderly writers have found new self-esteem and joy in rediscovering themselves.

Parents may wish to explore a particular hobby. A woman in a small rural California town makes "apple-head" dolls and dresses them in quaint, turn-of-the-century-style clothing.

Repeatedly she wins prizes for her creations.

A former shop teacher repairs, refinishes, recanes, and upholsters antique furniture for residents of a retirement village where he lives.

A 65-year-old San Diego "paper-woman" delivers a daily newspaper.

Hanna Meisner of West Lafayette, Indiana, worked to help the local Family Service Organizations establish a *Homemaker's Program* that sends homemakers to families— young and old—in need of household help.

An elderly couple in Cedar Rapids, Iowa, became professional baby-sitters. Living in a home when parents are away, they assume all household tasks and care of the children. In one 1½ year period they sat with 102 children from 31 families.

When Earl Knutson, Portland, a retired U.S. Army Corps Engineer, read about the Rent-a-Grandparent program, he decided to join them. He soon had a two-month backlog of work.

He says, "One little widow tells another about what I fixed for her, and my business grows. Most of my jobs are small—fixing a toilet, a stuck door, making a doorbell work. I do this mostly for people who can't afford 'professional prices.'"

Portland's Rent-a-Grandparent program was begun by another retiree, Loring Deming, 79, who had read about a similar project in New Mexico. Rent-a-Grandparent operates with a file card system containing names of elderly persons and their skills. Deming's office hours are from 8 a.m. to 4 p.m. Monday through Friday.

"When someone calls for a certain job," Deming says, "the staff checks that job heading and gives the caller the names and phone numbers of persons who can do the work. The workers set their own rates and ask for a minimum gas charge for work at a distance." [1]

A number of retired men in Akron, Ohio, find satisfaction in work that has for a long time been relegated to women—hospital volunteer work. Some greet and discharge patients; others visit them, listen to their complaints, or merely chat with them.

A Pennsylvania woman "critter-sits" for people's pets. A San Jose, California, woman "house-sits" for people who travel extensively.

Women around the country "adopt" men behind prison walls. They visit regularly, counsel, teach arts, crafts, and reading, whatever their "child" most needs. One young man said, "I trust my 'grandmother.' I tell her things I wouldn't tell anyone else. She's helping me shape up my life."

The above activities represent a mere wave on the ocean of quality involvement. You can help your parents select those they would like most to do.

The Church's Responsibility

What does your church do for elderly persons—your parents and other people's parents? Does it merely tolerate them, organize a Sunday school class, or plan recreational outings? These things have value. But is this enough?

Several elderly persons in our local church have opened their homes for Children's Neighborhood Bible Clubs.

Recently elderly persons served with the young in a hospitality program where groups of people (each including prospects, new members and old) met in a home for a potluck meal or an evening of fellowship. A woman in her 70s administered the program.

A group of elderly women tear sheets and roll bandages for missionaries in Zaire.

A retired banker keeps financial books for the church.

Nurses, some of whom are elderly, assist doctors in a well-baby clinic that meets monthly.

Some women show up at the church office asking, "What can I do to help?" Why not men?

Before his death a retired Des Moines businessman brought into the membership of the church over two hundred people annually through personal evangelism. Do you have a man with such ability sitting in the senior citizen's class of your church?

Some religious groups, the Salvation Army among them, plan day camps for the elderly. Ages of persons who attended one such gathering on a lake in Minnesota ranged from 60 to 87.

For the most part these campers represent a group of elderly who are often forgotten by the church. Frail, living alone, concerned about being a "bother," they never make known their need for a ride to church. They become "television church members," though they long for the fellowship of believers in their own church. If alerted to their need, church members could arrange to pick them up and return them to their homes each Sunday morning. A friend in St. Paul, Minnesota, has for several years taken a roundabout route to church so she can pick up elderly persons who have no car and do not live close to public transportation.

Members of a "cheer committee" could be responsible for calling on shut-ins regularly. As a special bonus they might circulate sermon, Bible study, and concert tapes among these people.

One church women's group arranges an annual luncheon when members over 75 are especially honored. In another church visits are made to all shut-ins on their birthdays.

Any older person may become involved in a telephone reassurance program, where, by telephone, volunteers contact assigned individuals to check on their health, chat, or to ask about personal needs.

A gerontologist at the Ethel Andrus Gerontology Center, Los Angeles, told me that his aged mother regularly rises at six o'clock each morning to telephone friends whom he calls her "pigeons." She stays on the phone until nine o'clock chatting, cheering, checking, or just listening to numerous problems and anxieties.

During the last years before retirement, a staff member for an international charitable association, Dorothy Haskin, Hollywood, California, traveled extensively throughout the world. The poverty she saw appalled her.

Once home, she began sending food packages to missionaries, who distributed them to especially needy people.

By the time she retired, she had 70 groups helping her, among them many elderly persons, in what she calls, "The Friendship Ministry." Volunteers contribute time, food, and money for shipping costs.

Quality of life also involves freedom from fear.

Safety in the Home

Your parents are apt to have more accidents than younger persons. They react more slowly, balance less ably. Regardless, you can help them by being aware of the following areas of danger.

* Rugs can be dangerous. Consequently no rug may be the best rug for them. Small throw rugs tend to slide and slip on a floor. Thick pile carpeting can cause an elderly person to stumble.

* Handrails. Staircases should be equipped with a handrail, preferably two, one on each side. Bathrooms need grab bars near the toilet and attached to or near the bathtub. Adhesive nonskid strips or a rubber bathmat should be used in the tub.

* Kitchen. Dishes and equipment should be accessible and easily reached. Provide reach-for tongs rather than a step stool for your parents. Realize electric stoves are safer than gas stoves. Encourage your parent to use a timer when food is being cooked.

* Smoke alarms. Purchase as many as necessary to protect your parents.

Crime

Fear of crime, someone has said, is more a problem than the crime itself for older persons. "The elderly are victims of personal attack less often than other age groups over 12 in the U.S.," Dr. Frank A. Clemente, Pennsylvania State University states. "Nevertheless, they are more afraid of crime and that fear forces them to curtail outside activities."[2]

Crime in Homes

Action for Independent Maturity, a division of AARP, has compiled a list of 10 precautions you and your parents should take to make their home safe.[3]

* Secure all locks (preferably dead locks and pinfall locks) on doors and windows. Homes should be kept locked even during the day.

* They ought not leave keys in a "hiding place"— mailbox or under a door mat.

* Outdoor lights should be kept on at night.

* Automatic timers should regulate inside lights while your parents are away from their home.

* If possible install a burglar alarm that sets off a noise, a floodlight, or both.

* Valuables need to be marked with an electric pencil available at police stations.

* The elderly should learn to know their neighbors. Then they can check on each other.

Crime on the Streets

Advise your parents to consider the following:

* Carry no money in their purses, only on their person.

* Insist that they not fight for a purse if it is snatched.

* Suggest they walk on the lighted, not the shaded side of the street.

* Make it possible for them not to have to go out alone at night.

* If one or both of your parents still drive, suggest they have their car keys in hand before they go to the car. And, that they always check the inside of the car before entering.

* In traveling by bus or some other public transportation, elderly persons should remain close-mouthed with

strangers. Purses should be watched carefully. Recently a young man left his seat to get off the bus. "Accidentally" he stepped down hard on a woman's foot. She turned in time to see he had opened her purse intent on stealing her billfold while she was distracted by the pain he caused.

An 80-year-old woman traveling several hundred miles by bus to see her son's family, left the bus and entered the station's rest room in one city. Once inside two women accosted her—one held the door shut while the other grabbed her purse, threw her to the floor and stomped on her, despite her cries, "Take the purse, but don't hurt me!"

Remarriage

Would you object to your father's remarriage? Conversely, to your mother's? Would you be judgmental? Fearful that your stepparent-to-be was only interested in the family estate? All of these factors need to be considered in the remarriage of a parent. In some instances character references *should be* checked if suspicion is aroused.

A considerate parent will discuss the new mate with you. He may ask you for assistance in arranging some kind of financial agreement, or in writing a new will. If he doesn't, you need not feel embarrassed about asking whether such agreements have been made and legally documented.

Some widows have been hoodwinked into a marriage that proved disastrous. This is not usually the case, however. An increasing number of older Americans are remarrying. Since 1960 the number has doubled, and that figure is due to rise since there will no longer be a Social-Security penalty for remarriage among the elderly after 1979. Studies reveal that 75 percent of all such remarriages are happy ones.

They aren't necessarily the story-book, starry-eyed type. More likely a relational marriage that provides mature, warm companionship. Stena and Carl had been friends for years. When both of their mates died, Stena, who has heart problems, and Carl, near-blind, married. Today, sharing a retirement center apartment, they compensate for each other's loss. A deep, warm companionship blesses their lives.

Don't assume, as some children do, that your parents are no longer interested in sex. Studies reveal that closeness evidenced in older marriages involves a good sex relationship. Yet the sex act may not be as significant as the awareness of closeness married couples enjoy.

From all indications the principles that make up a good marriage in youth hold true in "golden" marriages, too: a common faith; adequate finances; reputable characters; mutual interests.

Help Everywhere

As I've traveled in different areas of the country I've made it a point to pick up brochures that list services and activities available to the elderly. I've been astonished at the wide variety of material. If you have questions, check with a senior citizen group in your area. Use the telephone book to look up addresses and telephone numbers of organizations that serve the elderly. Ask for brochures that have been prepared for the area in which your parents live. Subscribe to *Modern Maturity,* a magazine which gives up-to-date information and news about the elderly.

7.

Money Matters

Money represents one of the touchiest areas in a son's or daughter's relationship with elderly parents. This is especially true in families where parents have never spoken freely about their economic status. When children were young, they may have feared they'd give away information other people should not know.

As parents age, they may continue this silence, fearing their children might not stand on their own feet if they know the extent of family assets.

Silence about finances can work a hardship, especially when a parent becomes ill. Children are torn between their own financial obligations and medical and institutional expenses they fear their parents cannot assume.

On the other hand, parents may be so frugal that they fail to take care of themselves, because they want to leave a sizeable "chunk" for their children. Children with integrity will discourage such action.

Money needs to be discussed, chiefly because it becomes more significant as people grow old. One must consider the probability that expenses during a parent's last years may exhaust all his savings.

If you haven't talked to your parents about finances previously, you may be reluctant to do so now. You fear they may feel you are after their money or that they aren't capable of handling their own affairs. Nevertheless, it's perfectly proper for you to discuss money with them. You will want to know if there is enough for living expenses in the forseeable future as well as for medical bills and long-time skilled nursing care.

If you feel confidently capable about assisting a parent in protecting his savings, you need not feel reluctant about doing so.

Protecting a Parent's Money

No matter how large or small their retirement savings, parents hope and pray it will be enough to supplement their Social Security and pension benefits and cover unforseen expenses.

Most money managers advise against spectacular growth investments as a person ages. The emphasis more frequently has to do with protection and maximum earnings instead. A friend in her 70s, who has for years been interested in growth stock, has now begun to convert her holdings into Savings and Loan Time Certificate deposits which may yield 7½ to 8¾ percent interest, depending on maturity date.

Others are investing in money-market mutual funds. Pioneered by Reserve Fund in 1971, these cash asset funds operate like a bank, except that investors buy their shares and obtain a higher rate of interest than they could on a passbook savings account.

These funds invest their money in relatively high-yielding bank Certificates of Deposit, banker's acceptances, and U.S. Government securities.

Because they are mutual funds they enable persons with moderate means who couldn't ordinarily afford to buy long-term government securities to do so. An added advantage: most money-market funds permit small-investment amounts with short-notice withdrawals. Check also the new, high interest 6-month or 1-year Treasury bond investments.

Insurance Policies

As a person ages he needs little insurance compared to the

amount needed when children were young. If a policy is paid-up it might be wise to investigate the redemption value to decide whether it pays to withdraw that amount and invest in savings certificates or some other interest-bearing program. Financial advisors can give you needed information.

Wills

Do advise your parents to consult an attorney and make a will designating where they wish their money to go when they are deceased. Since no one can predict the size of an elderly person's estate, urge them to apportion funds in percentages rather than in specific amounts.

Recently I took an elderly widow to the lawyer whom she wanted to make her will. I urged her to write down, beforehand, (1) exactly what she wanted to dispose of in her will; (2) the names of her beneficiaries and their addresses and relationships; (3) her choice of an executor, someone she could trust. Had she had extensive holdings, she might have prepared an inventory of all personal property, too.

If both parents are living they customarily leave most of their estate to the surviving spouse with a provision that indicates what should be done in the event of a "common disaster." This would involve apportioning percentages to surviving children. In many instances parents will want to leave a portion of the estate to their church, their denomination, its missionary work, or one of its institutions.

Wills need periodic review. Births, dates, and marriages necessitate changes. So does a move to another state.

Trusts and Annuities

One parent may worry about the ability of a spouse to handle large amounts of money. Trust funds can be set up or annuities purchased. Again urge your parent to see an attorney.

Employment

With retirement extended to 70 years, an ever-increasing number of people will opt for working a longer period of time. Thus retirement funds increase.

58

After retirement, part-time work or self-employment are options. A church custodian, recently retired, finds all the work he can handle. Once a week he cleans a neighbor's mobile home. He works early morning hours cleaning a furniture store.

A retired music teacher gives piano lessons to a select group of students—children and adults—who live in the vicinity of the retirement center where she resides.

Authors edit manuscripts for publishers; ghost write speeches and books; prepare newsletters for business, missionary, and philanthropic organizations. More likely, they continue their own writing.

A pastor's wife whose husband is retired does interior decorating for persons who wish this kind of assistance.

The opportunities are extensive if a parent has a particular skill and is well enough to work.

Economy

The elderly who suffer most in this day of spiraling cost are those in the moderate and low income brackets. If your parents belong in either group, alert them to economy measures that are available to them.

Food Stamp Eligibility

Applicants must meet nationwide standards of net income and resources. Though there has been a great deal of abuse of the program that provides supplementary resources for food purchasing, the elderly usually are not to blame. In fact, the food-stamp program has been dramatically underused by older people. An estimated 28 percent of the blind and disabled fail to participate in the program.

You may find your parents are eligible for food stamps. If so take them to your county welfare office and file an application. Be sure they take with them proof of income and expenditures.

Low Cost Meals

The federally subsidized Meals-on-Wheels program (not

available in all areas) provides for the delivery of modestly priced, nutritious meals to elderly persons who cannot leave their homes.

In some areas senior citizen centers and churches provide space and volunteer help needed to dispense similar meals to the mobile elderly.

Discount Privileges

Investigate transportation discounts in your locality. One of my neighbors, a widow in her 80s, takes advantage of "Dial-a-ride" van transportation for church, doctor, and shopping appointments.

If your parents live in a large city they may find buses charge less or no fee during nonrush periods of the day.

Many colleges discount tuition; some rent-a-car companies, as well as certain motels, give senior citizen discounts.

Many business firms and grocery stores specify days when 5 to 10 percent discounts are available.

Discriminate Spending

Alert parents to:

* End of the season sales when merchandise may be marked down as much as 25 or 50 percent.

* Drugs sold by their generic name can often be purchased for less than brand names. A doctor may indicate this preference on a prescription.

* Many banks provide free checking accounts and safety deposit boxes for the elderly.

* Thrift-store purchases. What one person discards another may be able to use.

* Day-old bakery purchases.

* Reduced telephone rates during early morning and late night hours as well as on weekends and holidays.

Frauds

Despite repeated warnings, elderly persons seem most vulnerable to frauds. Perhaps you will need to familiarize yourself with land frauds, bank deposit swindles, "pigeon drop" robberies, cheap mail-order moneymaking schemes that require a fee for information, and home improvement gyps so that you can explain attendant conniving and caution parents against falling victim to these schemes.

Management Protection

"Protection Service" is a term applied to legal services provided by the state agency for elderly persons, without family or relatives, who can no longer manage their own lives.

Lawyers and social workers assume such responsibility when an elderly person is unwilling or unable to protect his own interests, when he is mentally confused, when his behavior reveals mental, physical, and emotional incapacity to such an extent that he will harm himself when he can no longer manage his own money.

If you are the ones who must take over the management of your parents' finances, a lawyer may draw up a document that gives you the power of attorney and enables you to sign checks and manage whatever affairs are necessary in helping your parents.

In extreme instances of total incapability you may ask a court to appoint you a guardian or conservator for your parents. In these instances you will have greater control. Do this only as a last resort, however. It is a parent-demeaning procedure and one you should avoid as long as you can.

Parents may choose to place property in joint ownership with an only child long before management need be assumed. Often this is wise. There are instances, however, when a son or daughter has taken advantage of the arrangement to such an extent that the parent has little money on which to survive.

8.
Guardians of Health

You may think this chapter title implies that you who are adult children of aging parents are guardians of their health. This is not its intent. Unless they face serious financial difficulties, your involvement in the decisions of their lives is likely to be minimal *as long as they enjoy good health.* Yet, you stand ready to help them become good guardians of that health. In time you may, because of circumstances, be forced to assume the guardian role yourself.

Age Is Not a Disease

Do realize that old age is not in itself a disease, though there is a connection between age and disease. Elderly persons may suffer illnesses that speed the aging process. But these ailments aren't ordinarily acquired late in life. They may have been activated over a period of years.

In the past any coronary-artery disease was thought of as resulting from aging. World War II blasted that theory, however. Data gathered in 866 case studies of men 18 through 39 years of age who died of heart attacks revealed that 64 persons were under 24, over 200 under 29. Autopsies proved that coronary-artery changes were much the same in these individuals as found in elderly persons who died of heart attacks.[1]

Note, too, that hypertension, which used to be thought of as an "older" disease, is found in 10 percent of teenagers in some areas. Even younger children may be affected by high blood pressure. They also suffer from arthritis, diabetes, and kidney ailments.

We need to realize, however, that certain changes relevant only to aging do occur as a person grows old. Vision becomes less sharp; height diminishes; wrinkles appear. Hair thins and grays, and sleep patterns change. You, as I, have frequently heard older persons refer to such changes by comments such as, "I'm not as strong as I used to be. I tire more easily." Or, "I have a tendency to awaken very early each morning."

Lung capacity may be reduced, and bone deterioration occurs. Joints, especially hips and knees stiffen. Yet these changes can be slowed, in many instances halted. Diets often reverse fatigue and control diabetes. A regular program of exercise strengthens muscle tone; calcium improves bone density.

Medical Condescension

In his book, *Don't Give up on Your Aging Parents,* Lawrence Galton takes an almost angry stance against medical personnel who condescendingly appraise, or ignore, the health needs of the elderly.[2] For too long, he says, medical schools have failed to teach doctors how to care for the aging. Besides, doctors may, because they see only a small fraction of the total number of older people (chiefly those with acute health needs in hospitals and clinics), forget the large percentage who live productive, self-sufficient lives in community. They assume the 75- to 85-year-old invalid is "normal," the vigorous, "exceptional." The truth is that only a fraction of the over sixty-five are hospitalized or institutionalized.

Galton also feels that doctors may be so dedicated to "cures" that they feel threatened by older persons who keep on living with handicaps and illnesses without being cured.

Choosing a Doctor

Occasionally my husband and I are dinner guests at our

local retirement center. One day a resident, 90 years old, asked us to stop at his apartment for a magazine article he wanted us to have.

As we visited, I asked, "How are you feeling, Jim? Fully recovered from that bout with the flu?"

"I'm having a little trouble with my ears," he answered. "I don't know what to do."

"Seen a doctor?"

"Of course, and he sent me to a specialist. Trouble is I haven't gotten very much help. The specialist removed some wax from my ears, told me I could take this or that type of medication. Yet he didn't write a prescription. Said I should go home and think about it for two weeks, then come in again. 'But what is there to think about?' I asked. 'I'm not a professional.' Well, just go home home and think about it, he said. I wouldn't go back to that man if. . . ."

Blame Jim? I don't. I'd find myself another ear doctor, and that speedily.

Despite his age, Jim is perfectly capable of doing that. There may come a time when your parents, too, may feel they are not being treated correctly. Or their doctor may have retired or died. Whichever, they may want to find someone else to care for them. Help them, if they ask you to.

It's always wise to speak to the new doctor about a parent's needs prior to an appointment. And you can insist on being present at a first interview. Later if you have questions about care, don't hesitate to call for information. Expect the doctor to be honest and forthright.

Suppose your parents plan a move to a new locality. They may wonder how to find a good doctor. You can suggest that they ask their former doctor for a recommendation. He may name a medical school classmate or a medical society colleague who lives in the area to which your parents move. Or you or your parents can contact medical schools, county and state medical societies. Be aware, too, that a pastor or a nurse is as capable as many to judge a doctor's interest and capability in caring for the elderly.

When you communicate with your parents' doctor from a

distance, make use of your telephone. Call person-to-person. Should the doctor be busy, you can leave your number and ask that he call you collect at his convenience.

Before you make that call, however, make a list of specific questions you want answered. If a doctor couches his answers in technical terms you don't understand ask for explanations in laymen terms. Should surgery be contemplated, encourage your parent to seek a second opinion. And do suggest that costs and ability to pay be discussed prior to, not after, an operation.

Hospital Care

Describing his hospital care experiences, one man wrote, "The last place anyone should be sick is in a hospital." To an extent he is right. Pain, discomfort, and calls for attention are often ignored in busy hospitals. If your parent is hospitalized, don't assume all is well. Do some investigating.

Check:

* Room. Is it clean, well ventilated and heated? Older persons whose circulation is poor often suffer from cold and need more heat than the average person.

* Regular professional attention. Does a nurse, doctor, intern, resident, or aid check regularly on progress, regression, medication, bowel movements, and urination? Does the doctor do more than say, "Hi, how are you today? I'll see you on my next round."

* Food. Is food nutritious and good? Are special diets observed?

* Medication. Are drugs carefully monitored? Does your parent receive the drugs prescribed? Does the person who dispenses the drug note *for sure* that the medication is taken? Are side effects noted and properly corrected?

* Doctor's orders. Are they relayed accurately? Mistakes can be made. Here's one from my own experience.

One morning before scheduled surgery, a nurse came into my hospital room intent on giving me an enema.

"Oh, no you don't," I told her.

"Doctor's orders," she answered.

"I disagree."

"Well," she retorted angrily. "We'll see about that." She picked up the chart at the end of my bed. Instantly her face flamed. "You . . . you had one yesterday," she stammered. "And you are scheduled for surgery today? Someone must have forgotten to change the orders at the desk."

* Treatment. Are patients demeaned? You don't need to be suspicious of everyone who cares for a parent. Nevertheless, don't ignore your parent's complaints. Check them out. They may be valid.

I have found that hospitals operated by religious organizations dispense the most reliable, loving and tender care. One summer I spent five weeks with a daughter who had been taken to a Catholic hospital following a tragic automobile accident. I'm extremely grateful for the compassionate concern shown by nurses involved in her intensive care and for the kindness, patience, and perseverance of rehabilitation therapists.

As diligent, my own denomination's local hospital is known for miles around for its love, care, and professional integrity.

Diseases of the Elderly

In my book, *Looking Ahead—the Realities of Aging; Face them with Faith,*[3] I describe in detail the various diseases with which elderly persons are afflicted. I will recap this information briefly here, giving most attention to cardiovascular diseases, cancer, and strokes, which cause death most frequently, so that you can learn to identify their symptoms and suggest needed care.

Hypertension

When a doctor diagnoses a person's problem as hypertension, he isn't talking about anxiety and stress. He's using the medical term for high blood pressure. The most prevalent chronic disease in America, hypertension is an abnormality in the pressure exerted to pump blood through the body.

People with high blood pressure experience three times as many heart attacks as those with normal blood pressure. Strokes are four times more likely, and congestive heart problems five times. Besides, the incidence of kidney failure is greatly increased.

Though hypertension may exist without a person being aware of it, light-headedness, dizziness, sleeplessness, shortness of breath, vision problems, heart palpitations, and swelling of the ankles may indicate its presence.

Fortunately medication can control high blood pressure. Many doctors also restrict the use of salt, caffeine, refined sugar, and animal fat. A Tufts' Medical School alumnus claims that in a Harvard University study of tribal groups in the Solomon Islands, salt was identified as the single greatest cause of high blood pressure.[4]

Heart Diseases

Hypertension and artherosclerosis (hardening of the arteries) carry the blame for most heart disease. Artherosclerosis—a form of arteriosclerosis, describes a condition where fatty deposits and calcium clog artery channels. When this happens, blood coagulates and forms a clot (a thrombus) which cuts off blood flow and robs the heart of needed oxygen so that it no longer functions properly. Then the victim has a heart attack.

Occasionally a heart attack is so slight a person may not have felt it. Most attacks, however, occur accompanied by excruciating pain that strikes the center of the chest and radiates through the left arm, shoulder, neck and jaw. The victim feels he is unable to breathe. He pales, becomes nauseated, and may lose consciousness.

Since immediate attention is imperative, you should advise your parents to grab a phone and call their doctor at once if they suspect one or the other is suffering an attack. Or urge them to call an ambulance, the fire department, or police department. The object is to get to the hospital as speedily as possible and insist on instant attention.

One morning a friend, Lona, age 64, awakened at 6 o'clock in the morning with a crushing pain in her chest. Unable to breathe, she thought she was dying. And well she may have.

Her sister called a doctor who lived a block away. He hastened to the girls' home and began pulmonary resuscitation (CPR) until an ambulance arrived. Within minutes Lona was receiving emergency care that spared her life.

Daniel C. Brown and other investigators of the UCLA Medical School have discovered that coughing every one-and-one half seconds can alleviate dangerous rhythm disturbances. "It's conceivable," Dr. Brown reports, "that this technique could have wide applicability among cardiac patients at high risk of sudden death. A patient, recognizing that he was going into ventricular fibrillation—that sinking feeling—could cough his way to a phone and call for help and continue coughing until help arrived."[5]

Different types of heart attacks require varied treatment. If a parent suffers from angina pectoris, a condition attributed to the same cause as a coronary thrombosis, a reduced amount of blood continues to reach the heart. Usually this condition subsides quickly if nonaddictive nitroglycerine tablets are placed under the tongue the moment pain is felt. It's important that persons who suffer these attacks make sure they always carry a fresh supply of tablets, in a container they are able to open easily and speedily.

You may recall the *Reader's Digest* story that told about a man, who after his father's funeral, went to the spot where his father had suffered a heart attack. There he found a badly smashed plastic bottle containing nitroglycerine tablets. Unable to remove the cover, the elderly man had tried unsuccessfully with a rock to break the bottle.

Congestive heart attacks occur when the heart's ability to pump blood has been curtailed by circulatory disease or by damage to the heart structure. Blood backs up in the veins, causing congestion in body tissues. Fluids accumulate, chiefly in legs and ankles, breathing becomes difficult.

Rest and drugs that eliminate fluids are required. Digitalis may be prescribed to strengthen heart muscles.

Today surgery saves the lives of many persons who formerly would have succumbed to heart disease of one kind or another. Coronary artery bypass surgery, a procedure in which a section of a patient's leg vein is grafted onto a diseased coronary artery to detour circulation around a blocked or severely diseased area, is used extensively today. Also, pacemakers, tiny electronic devices, are inserted to stimulate heart action when the heart cannot function on its own. New heart valves can be inserted to function for those that are badly damaged.

A National Institute of Health study, Massachusetts General Hospital, Boston, indicates that age in itself ought no longer be regarded as a reason not to operate. Seventy-three persons, 60 to 77 years of age, who underwent valve replacement were compared with 277, 12 to 59 years of age who had similar surgery. Hospital death rate in the elderly was actually only half that of younger patients; later death rate was no higher, and improvement in both groups was nearly identical.[6]

In spite of surgical success, cardiac experts urge elderly patients not to rush into surgery unless a condition is considered an emergency. Of all heart operations the one presently causing the most controversy is the coronary-artery bypass. The operation is popular. Surgeons report long waiting lists of patients eager to undergo the operation, even though it may cost as much as $12,000.

A recent study by the Veterans Administration has led to skepticism regarding its usefulness. The study shows that a coronary bypass may in some instances be no more effective in prolonging life than standard medical treatment with drugs.

Other investigators counter this criticism, claiming that a

coronary bypass not only lengthens life but improves the quality of it. It relieves angina pain, while patients treated with drugs still suffer from chest pains.

Recently I met a 79-year-old woman who had an emergency coronary bypass. She was elated with the results. "It's like being given a second life," she said.

Strokes

Strokes, vascular accidents, which may affect young adults, are most common among the elderly. Hardening of the arteries or other blood diseases cause them. Sometimes a blood vessel that has lost its elasticity breaks as a result of suddenly increased blood pressure, extreme physical exertion, or severe emotional stress. Or a blood clot may be responsible. A stroke's mildness or severity is determined by the size of the broken vessel or clot and its location in the brain. Warning signals include: dizziness, acute headaches, slurred speech. Though a stroke may be fatal, lost mobility can often be restored by medication and therapy.

Since strokes can be postponed, in some instances, prevented, urge your parents to have their blood pressure and cholesterol count checked periodically.

Cancer

Cancer, man's most dreaded disease because of the devastation it causes, involves irrational, purposeless growth of cells. It invades and destroys other tissues and by cutting off blood supply destroys them. In a process known as metastasis, cancer can establish growths far removed from the original cancer cells.

Cancer may be treated by surgery, radiation, or chemotherapy. Statistics indicate that a very high percentage of cancers, particularly certain types, can be cured if detected and properly treated in time.

Since speedy diagnosis is of utmost importance, your parents need to be alert to cancer warnings: unusual bleeding or discharge, a lump or thickening in the breast or other parts of the body; a change in normal bladder or bowel functions; a sore which refuses to heal; continued hoarseness; persistent indigestion; difficulty in swallowing; a change in the size and color of a mole.

Diabetes

A condition where abnormal amounts of sugar are discovered in the blood or urine, diabetes indicates a failure on the part of the pancreas to produce enough insulin to allow the blood to store and properly utilize sugar.

Abnormal thirst, the passage of large amounts of urine, obesity, loss of strength, and, in some cases, loss of weight, may indicate the presence of diabetes. Though it cannot be cured, *in some instances* it can be controlled by insulin injections, diabetic tablets, or low-sugar diets.

A diabetic parent should be told that diabetes aggravates artherosclerosis, and if not treated properly can harm circulation and precipitate the amputation of a limb.

Emphysema

This disease causes lungs to lose their elasticity and their ability to exhale all the carbon dioxide they should. Consequently space for life-sustaining oxygen is stolen.

As the disease progresses, the tiny air sacs inflate like balloons and burst. Complications may result in death.

Doctors name cigarette smoking and possibly air pollution as causes of the disease. A parent who smokes should be encouraged to stop.

Arthritis

The number one crippler, arthritis, affects millions of people in our country. Yet, early diagnosis and care prevent crippling in seven out of ten cases.

Osteoarthritis results from wear and tear on the joints. Heat, braces, aspirin, cortisone injections, and other drugs may be used to relieve pain.

Rheumatoid arthritis, which attacks the young as well as the old, cripples most severely. It causes joints to swell and become painful, eventually to stiffen and deform. Fever, muscle weakness, and weight loss are common. Here, too, aspirin (the leading arthritis medication), cortisone, and other drugs are used to relieve pain. Increasingly surgery repairs deformed feet, hand, hip, and knee joints. Age doesn't seem to be a factor. Persons as old as 80 or 90 have recovered and been freed from pain through this type of surgery.

Eye Diseases

Your parents should be encouraged to have their eyes checked regularly. Glaucoma and cataracts are the most common eye ailments of the elderly. Glaucoma, all 45 varieties, have one thing in common. Drainage inside the eye is impaired so abnormal pressure builds up and curtails blood supply, causing damage to the peripheral nerves. Tunnel vision results.

A doctor who diagnoses glaucoma will prescribe eye drops that must be used with conscientious regularity.

The lens, a flexible transparent pale yellow protein behind the colored iris of a normal eye, adjusts to focus images on the retina. When the lens clouds and obstructs light, an elderly person can suspect cataracts. Surgery involving the removal of the lens, together with corrective glasses, can remedy this condition.

Hearing Problems

If your parents become noticeably hard of hearing, encourage them to see an audiologist, who will determine whether hearing loss is caused by an excessive buildup of wax or by some physical defect. If the latter case, the specialist will determine whether surgery or a hearing aid is needed.

If a hearing aid is needed, an audiologist can suggest the type he believes would be most beneficial. It is wise, however, for an elderly person to try several types before making a purchase. Fortunately the Federal Trade Commission has made a 30-day trial period possible. If the customer is not satisfied his money should be refunded.

Some people have the mistaken notion that prolonged use of a hearing aid increases loss of hearing. A study made by the Veterans Administration Hospital, Tucson, Arizona, has proved this to be a false concept.[7]

Though some elderly persons find it difficult to cope with illness, others manage very well by compensating for health loss. Take the parent who is partially blind, for instance. He turns to large-print reading material and talking records. He may learn Braille. One who is deaf begins to rely more keenly on his eyesight. The hard-of-hearing buys a hearing aid or submits to an ear operation. The arthritic curtails activity, turns to more sedentary recreation and work. He may arrange for an operation that promises help. A person who suffers memory loss learns to keep a pencil and pad handy to jot down whatever he needs to recall.

Fortunately high blood pressure and obesity are less threatening as people grow older. Cancer, too, we have learned, progresses more slowly in elderly bodies than in those that are young.

9.

Nutrition/Exercise/Drugs

* An acquisition editor of a large publishing house told me how shocked he and his brothers were when doctors discovered their mother was suffering from severe malnutrition.

  "We often enquired about their eating," he said. "We'd ask, 'Do you prepare nourishing meals? Do you eat regularly?'

  "'Surely,' she'd answer, and from all appearances she was telling the truth. We checked food supplies periodically, invited her out for meals. Everything seemed in order. But it wasn't."

* Recently I spent several days visiting a patient in a health care center in the central part of the United States. I socialized with the patients, ate with them, and observed their daily routine.

  In the dining room before breakfast they were put through a series of stay-seated exercises. Arms above head; up; down; to the right; to the left. Head turned to the right; back; to the left. Knees lifted to reach the table; one; two. Good, I thought, here is concern about exercise.

  Then rising early one morning I noted that the nonmobile were brought, one by one in the order in which they were dressed, in wheelchairs to a central lounge where they watched television until breakfast was called.

They were returned to the lounge after breakfast, joined by those who could walk and occupy more comfortable chairs. But there most of them sat until dinner, and again until supper—watching one channel's schedule of programs. When they wanted to nap they merely allowed their heads to fall onto their shoulders. I did note, however, that a few were returned to their rooms for a bed nap.

* A Miami, Florida, woman was hospitalized because of depression and disorientation. After a series of tests, the family learned her condition was caused by a drastic reaction to the medications that weren't compatible to each other.

The first of these three illustrations points up the importance of good nutrition in an elderly parent's life; the second hints of need for various types of exercise; the third, speaks to the importance of monitoring drugs for the aged.

Nutrition

There may have been several reasons why the editor's mother wasn't eating properly. It could be that she had lost her zest for cooking. Food had always been associated with eager hungry children; family gatherings; surprise parties. Food was a medium by which she expressed love for her family. Now she just didn't feel like preparing a meal that included meat, bread, vegetables, milk, and a salad. This can be true when a parent lives alone or with a spouse.

Nutritionally a widower may fare worse than a widow. Most men haven't the slightest idea of all that is involved in meal preparation. They opt for convenience foods, toast and coffee, wieners and buns, whatever. Education is needed. You can help your father, if he is alone, by making a map of the grocery store so that he knows exactly where items can be found. Buy him a basic cook book. Suggest he visit the center which provides subsidized nutritional meals for the mobile elderly. If one or both of your parents are housebound, arrange for meals-on-wheels to be delivered once a day.

A Michigan survey of 300 over-sixty residents revealed that only two-thirds had eaten three meals on the day before the interviews. It also indicated that 17 percent had had no more than three basic foods required for a balanced diet.[1]

Nutritional Checklist

The daily nutritional needs of your elderly parents are much the same as yours, except that they may not need as much food as you and special diets may need to be prescribed. Some doctors encourage five smaller meals a day rather than three of normal size. Each day's menu should include:

* 2 or more glasses of milk. Cheese, ice cream and other milk-containing foods can supply part of that amount.

* 2 or more servings of meat, fish, poultry, eggs or cheese. Use dry beans, peas, or nuts as alternates.

* 4 or more servings of vegetables and fruits. Dark green or yellow vegetables and citrus fruits and tomatoes should be included.

* 4 or more servings of enriched grain breads and cereals.

It's important that your parents eat a varied diet. The greater their choice of foods, the less chance that they will miss essential nutrients. They should understand that fried foods, highly seasoned foods, starchy foods, and foods that contain large amounts of animal fat, gravies and heavy sauces, are hard to digest. Fat should be trimmed from meat. Poultry, which is high in protein, is low in fat.

Fruits, vegetables, and foods with fiber and bulk help prevent constipation.

Plenty of fluids prevents dehydration and aids digestion.

Older persons should go easy on salt. It tends to accelerate blood pressure. An alternative: vinegar, lemon juice, and some spices.

Though sugar makes food more palatable, excessive amounts are harmful. According to Linus Pauling, Nobel Prize winner for his work in chemistry, people who consume up to 120 pounds of sugar per year have six times the chance of getting a coronary heart disease as those who consume 60 pounds or less.

Food Supplements

One of the great ironies of our day is that the more sophisticated the processing of food becomes, the more warnings we hear about how nutritional values may be reduced in the process. Actually this has become a matter of great controversy. In all, about 3,000 additives are now in use. Some convenience foods are mainly sugar, additives, and synthetic vitamins. This is true of one brand of imitation orange juice. In some instances additives are used to thicken diet drinks, canned milk, baby formula, preserves, and cheaper grades of ice cream. Some food colors have been banned from the market. Advise your parent to learn which they are and to read carefully the labels of purchased food.

Speaking about nutrition, some people claim it is possible to obtain all the nourishment we need from food products alone. Others fear that valuable nutrients are eliminated when food is refined or processed for consumption. The result of such fears, both legitimate and exaggerated, have triggered a phenomenal growth in the dispensing of "health foods." While many of the highly advocated "organic" and "natural" products are nutritious, people have been led to believe they are superior to other foods. Some so-called "organic" products and packaged foods are not organic at all. In 1971, the Connecticut Protection Department found that of seven foods so advertised, six had spray residues.[2]

Definitions

The President's Office of Consumer Affairs places these definitions on foods (that health food buyers usually accept):

"Natural Foods" are products marketed without preservatives, emulsifiers, or artificial ingredients.

77

"Organic food," essentially like "natural," implies that they were raised without pesticides and chemical fertilizers.

"Health foods" include not only organic and natural, but dietetic, vegetarian, and other products, some of which contain artificial chemicals.

Problem

Problems arise when people are led to believe certain foods are miracle foods. Realize there are no miracle foods. The best nutrition cannot keep anyone young forever, slim a person without effort, eradicate all fatigue or all headaches. Nor does diet prevent arthritis, multiple sclerosis, or muscular dystrophy.

Warnings

To protect us against faddists, Jean Mayer, Professor of Nutrition, Harvard University, has offered the following suggestions:[3]

Be wary of any magic substance that will solve all of our problems. Realize excessive use of vitamin D causes calcification. Large doses of vitamin A can cause bleeding and bone fragility.

The use of too much vitamin C over a long period of time can cause a burning feeling during urination and can lead to small kidney stones.

Interest in lecithin, heralded as a miracle substance in the 1950s, has been revived. Some 20 years ago scientists discovered that when lecithin was injected into the body, cholesterol deposits in artery walls were decreased. However, lecithin by mouth had no such effect.

Despite this knowledge, lecithin tablets are being promoted as a miracle cure for cholesterol and strokes.

Nutritionist, Elizabeth Gunnear, believes lecithin does help clear vessels of cholesterol deposits. "But," she says, "they are absorbed by blood vessels, causing them to harden and loose their elasticity. Certainly not a remedial procedure."

Wheat germ, a useful food and a good source of vitamins E and B, contains the same nutrients as a diet high in fruits, vegetables, vegetable oils, and whole cereals.

Honey, contrary to modern beliefs, has few nutrients. (Baby bees get their nutrients from pollen and their calories from honey.) Honey can be as disastrous on teeth as sugar.

A great deal of attention has surfaced recently regarding hypoglycemia (low blood sugar). Some people, because they feel tired and depressed, have come to believe they have the disease. They forget that fatigue can result from diabetes, cancer, hepatitis, pernicious anemia, iron deficiency, and many other sources and that only a doctor can diagnose the cause. If you suspect low blood sugar, ask your doctor for a glucose tolerance test.

I never thought anyone would assume the presence of hypoglycemia until a friend told me she had diagnosed the disease herself. Had a doctor confirmed her diagnosis? No, he had said she didn't have the disease, but she was sure that was what was troubling her.

Dr. Mayer says, "The faddists would have everyone believe that anything that is natural is good. 'Natural Vitamins' have the same arrangement of atoms as those in a laboratory, and all atoms are natural."

My personal quarrel with some promoters of "natural vitamins and food supplements" is the exorbitant prices they charge. Were an elderly parent on a limited budget to buy them and take them in the large daily doses recommended, he'd be strapped to buy the nutritious groceries he needs.

I do not mean to imply that vitamins aren't helpful when needed. Vitamin B has alleviated numerous causes of fatigue, weakness, confusion, and anemia.

Vitamin C can alleviate bone tenderness and bruises. Because calcium absorption deceases with age, additional amounts may be needed. And because the elderly often neglect nutritional needs, doctors often prescribe a daily supplementary multiple-vitamin.

You can learn a great deal about well-balanced, nutritious meals and how to prepare them by reading Virginia and Norman Rohrer's book, *How to Eat Right and Feel Great.*[4] I also recommend a cookbook that is helpful economically as well as nutritionally: *The More-with-Less Cookbook* by Doris Janzen Longacre (Herald Press).

Exercise

Though I described a situation where I sensed a lack of sufficient exercise, perhaps because of a limited staff, I must admit that I have discovered excellent programs in many places. The Westside Jewish Community in Los Angeles is a good example. Persons suffering from arthritis start with warm-up exercises in the gymnasium, followed by a wide variety of exercises in a swimming pool where people with many ailments participate. Those who wish to stay dry, do poolside exercises, they bend, twist, kick, and do pushups.

A televised documentary of such a program told of 60-, 70-, 80-, and 90-year-old persons whose lives had been revitalized and illnesses alleviated through exercise.

A senator reporting to the Senate Committee on Aging said he had watched a group of older persons, 65 to 85, participate in vigorous calisthenics. Some suffered from chronic conditions, others from acute physical disabilities.

Among the group was a woman, 72, who having broken both legs and being told she would never be able to bend one knee or walk again, moves around with ease.

A man, 81, who two years previously had been incapacitated by a spinal operation, walks unassisted.[5]

Though the elderly person living in his own home may not have access to such programs, he can follow exercise programs on television, ride a stationary bicycle, jump rope (start slowly here).

Gardening is good exercise.

Some older persons walk, others jog. Admittedly, the most profitable exercise is a brisk walk. A 75-year-old retired minister walks 2, 3, and sometimes 4 miles a day.

Moderate, sustained exercise has both a direct and an indirect effect on diabetes. Exercise reduces weight and, in the early stages of the disease before insulin becomes necessary, improves glucose tolerance—sometimes to the point of complete remission.

Dr. J. Norris, who did a study of coronary disease among English postmen, learned that sedentary mail clerks had a higher mortality rate than delivery men, who walked extensively.

The elderly people in the Caucasus, Kashmir, and Ecuador, noted for their longevity, live extremely active lives well into their 90s.

At the University of California 96 volunteers, 66 to 87 years of age, participated in a test exercise program. Beginning cautiously, they exercised three times a week, about an hour at a time. At the end of six weeks they showed marked improvement—a 6 percent drop in blood pressure, a 9 percent improvement in oxygen intake.

Psychological Benefits

A regular exercise program relieves tension and pentup aggression. It offers the pleasure of social contacts. It alleviates insomnia, restlessness, feelings of panic, and muscle tension. Someone has said exercise is better than tranquilizers.

Having learned the benefits of exercise, you may be wondering how you can nudge a parent into such a program. I suggest you join him. Take walks, jog, do calisthenics, bowl, swim, whatever, with him. His health will be improved; so will yours.

Drugs

It has been estimated there are more than 7,000 drugs being marketed today. Though many are valuable, often lifesaving, they can cause problems. Some 500,000 persons a year are admitted to hospitals because of drug abuse. In one hospital 30 percent of the patients had been admitted because of drug-induced ailments.

If your parent is taking prescription drugs, you will want to learn how they are being used and for what purpose. Check with your parent's doctor. Learn the nature of the drug and if it is really needed. Ask if it has possible side effects and how they can be recognized. When several drugs are being used, find out if they are compatible.

Side Effects

Few people know to what extent frequently used and commonly helpful drugs can cause side effects. Drugs prescribed for hypertension, for instance, may cause nausea, vomiting, loss of appetite, diarrhea, itching, skin rash, ulcers, impotence, muscle pains, and a susceptibility to colds.

Cortisone drugs administered for arthritis may cause skin and allergy reactions, excess hair, diabetes aggravation, vertigo, headaches, and increased blood pressure.

Almost any drug may produce side effects, as may any substance taken into the body under certain conditions and varying sensitivities. With some individuals celery and strawberries cause hives.

Because their bodies do not break down and eliminate some drugs as do bodies of younger persons, the elderly may suffer more side effects. Persons with weak bladders may be bothered by urine retention when taking drugs for gastrointestinal problems. Certain antidepressants and tranquilizers have the same effect.

Interaction

When one man who had been treated with an anticoagulant drug returned home, he ceased taking the phenobarbital he had taken in the hospital. Without the sedative the dose of anticoagulant became an overdose and thinned his blood to a danger point.

Aspirin, too, may interact with an anticoagulant and cause bleeding.

Nose drops may affect heartbeat. Alcohol with drugs depresses the central nervous sytem, sometimes to such an extent that it kills.

Overdose

An elderly parent may feel that if one pill is good, two or three may be that much more effective. A parent who is forgetful may lose track of time and the number of pills or the amounts of medication he has taken.

A Rochester, Minnesota, study involving 101 patients on

digitalis found that 34 admitted they had missed one dose of medication during a six-month period. Blame was placed on forgetfulness, lack of money for refills, fear of overdose, and mistaken belief the medication wasn't need.

Outdated Medication

Together with a parent make a periodic check of his medicine chest. Note the date medications were prescribed and ask your parent to discard outdated medicine. Loss of potency can cause severe reactions.

Self-Prescribed Drugs

It is not surprising, considering the constant touting of numerous sleeping pills, back-pain medications, laxatives, and tonics that the elderly are enticed to buy and try medications they don't need and which may cause harm. Be aware of over-the-counter drugs your parents are taking. Caution against such practice if you need to.

10.
When Behavior Changes

It's natural for you to feel bewildered and distressed when a parent's behavior begins to change. For it is at this point that you enter a new phase of responsibility.

If you do not understand these changes, you may wish to consult a professional. Be wary, however, when such an individual says, "This is to be expected. It's nothing but old age, and there's nothing you can do about it."

That's far too simplistic an answer. There may be things you can do about it. Erratic behavior, whatever its form, has many causes. Here are a few: physical illness, mental illness, emotional trauma, a severe shock. Besides, there are factors that originate out of the events and relationships of a person's past life that also trigger change. They may cause you to say, "I just don't understand my mother anymore. She complains about everything." Or, "My dad thinks I'm trying to steal his money."

Change Through Loss

According to Barbara Silverstone and Helen Kandel Hyman,[1] the triggering of change has one overall cause, *loss*. Some losses may be obvious, and you can respond sympathetically to them. For instance, you'd expect your widowed mother to mourn the loss of your father. You'd understand life is miserable for a father who is arthritic and expresses concern about his pain.

Other losses may not be as understandable. Largely because you tend to look at life *as you would react to it.*

You no doubt know that cellular and tissue changes affect the nervous system and curtail sensitivity and perceptual abilities. All of us lose some of the eight to ten billion neurons (brain cells) that enable us to store and retrieve information and control body functions.

Most people grow old with enough neurons intact until the time comes when they suffer from some disease or accident that results in death. They manage to cope very well with little behavior change in spite of multiple losses. Others have problems coping. The attitudes of your parents, their psychological makeup, and personality traits determine to a large extent how they will fare.

A parent who suffers a severe stroke may have to be placed in a nursing home. Though he suffers social isolation as well as pain, he may accept his lot without grumbling. Deaf and blind people also feel isolation. Afflicted persons accept their lot differently, according to each one's individual makeup.

Loss of financial security may cause a normally complacent parent to worry about his future. He may fear his money will not reach. He may constantly inquire about his assets, even accuse a son or daughter of mismanagement of funds.

Suppose your mother's pet parakeet dies. She refuses to be comforted. "But," you say, "it's nothing but a bird."

Not to her. Recently, in the company of a group of Arizona women, I listened to an older woman, a retired educator, tell how badly she felt when a parakeet she had taught to talk died of old age. I've heard since tht she relates over and over again the events of her life as they pertain to the bird. She mourns its death as a mother would mourn the loss of a child.

Professionals might rationalize that she is linking this loss to one far more traumatic that occurred years ago.

Look, too, at the parent who because of his age has been forced into a life of idleness. He may become extremely critical of his business successor. Bitterness may replace former compassion. You may not be able to understand why he doesn't keep busy with other activities.

Adult children often overract in such situations. Pressing upon a parent some hobby or job assignment to keep him occupied may make him angry rather than appreciative. In instances where adult children must take over the management of a parent's finances, they too often withhold information which, if explained in detail, could smooth ruffled feathers.

Depression

No one knows exactly why or how a person goes into a state of depression. We Americans have often been called a yo-yo emotional society. In a sense this designation is correct. All of us have our ups and downs, periods when we feel low and periods when we feel we could conquer the world. Depression as a mental disorder represents a different mood game. It isn't temporary or fluctuating, but sustained.

This prolonged down feeling may be brought on by many causes. Tim LaHaye calls attention to seven causes in his book *How to Win over Depression.*[2] I'll list those I believe pertain to the elderly:

* *Disappointment.* No one becomes depressed when everything is going well. High hopes may have been shattered. Children may have let a parent down. They may have become neglectful. Many parents have waited endlessly for a promised visit, only to have a son or daughter call with some flimsy excuse for not keeping his or her word.

* *Low self-esteem.* A parent may say, "I can't do anything right anymore. I'm no good to anyone. I'm just a bother. I wish I were dead." Coupled with lack of self-esteem is the feeling of unfulfillment—of not having attained one's goals.

* *Unfair Comparison.* Again related to lack of esteem, comparing oneself with another can cause despondency. Remember King David admitted, "I was envious . . .

when I saw the prosperity of the wicked" (Ps. 73:3).

* *Ambivalence.* Some psychiatrists say this is the most common cause of depression. It involves a feeling of being trapped, unable to remedy an intolerable situation. I recall hearing my husband tell of visiting a man who was confined to a nursing home only because he was in a wheelchair. Trapped and extremely despondent, with no chance of escape, he said, "I'd be happy living in a barn if I had someone to live with me. It's hard to be cooped up in this little room."

* *Sickness.* Every person has a breaking point. Prolonged intensive pain can be devastating. At one time in my life when I had the "weeps," a doctor said, "I believe your body has reached its limit in tolerance of pain." What he said proved true.

* *Biological malfunction.* Thyroid problems, low blood sugar, or chemical changes of one kind or another can trigger depression.

* *Rejection.* A pastor visited a woman who, he had heard, was extremely depressed. He found her arranging a lovely bouquet of roses. "How nice," he said. "Is this a special day? A birthday?"

The woman nodded. Then she burst into tears.

The pastor asked, "Are the flowers from one of your children?"

"From my son." She shook her head sadly. "But, I'd rather have him."

"Where does your son live?"

"Right here, in this very town." she answered, then in an effort to tone down her disappointment, she added, "He's so busy."

From this list you will have noted that depression evolves from both external and internal causes. Whichever, it is important that you learn to recognize accompanying symptoms: withdrawal, sadness, irritability, erratic sleep, apathy, headaches, loss of appetite, anxiety, a feeling of hopelessness, frequent periods of weeping.

In some instances severely depressed individuals insist their problems are physical when they aren't. They hide behind what are known as "somatic" masks. Don't assume this is true of your parents when and if they become depressed, however. Check for cause to make sure.

In our youth-oriented society many older people feel a loss of status, a sense of uselessness. They feel unwanted. They panic when old friends pass away. They fear becoming ill and infirm. Whether these feelings are justified or not, they can, in many instances, be reversed by reassurances and lavishly apportioned evidences of love.

Depression proved to be the underlying problem of an elderly woman who lived with a busy, self-centered daughter whose very attitude demeaned her mother. After several months, a sister took the woman into her home. In a warm, loving setting where reassurance and concern were common, she recovered and regained her self-esteem.

Everyone doesn't respond as readily, however. Today antidepressant drugs properly prescribed and utilized can counter depression, often terminate it. Don't look for sudden cures, however. It may take weeks for drug therapy to prove effective.

In cases of very extreme depression electric shock coupled with psychiatry may be necessary to improve a person's mental outlook.

If your parent is depressed, you may be thinking, "But Dad's a Christian. Why should he be depressed?"

I heard a similar comment in a Bible class not long ago. Too often, one man suggested, depression may evolve from attacks by the Enemy. A Spirit-filled person ought not succumb.

I'm fully aware that Satan does attack. He did in Job's case.[3] I'm aware, too, that spiritual stagnation can cause a downward spiral. Seeking God's forgiveness and help in these instances is imperative. I know persons who have been healed of depression through prayer and a turning back to God.

Nevertheless, the mind and body are vulnerable and when extreme stress fences one in to such an extent that despair results, handle with care. Pray, yes, but seek outside help, too, if necessary. Remember, great men and women from all walks of life have suffered depression. The elderly are especially vulnerable, as is indicated by the number who, in despair, commit suicide.

Forgetfulness

Someone has likened the subconscious mind to an attic where all the paraphernalia of a lifetime has been stored. Suddenly forced to retrieve an article we need, we flounder, unable to locate it instantly.

Everyone is forgetful at times. We ask, "Where did I put that letter?" "I'm supposed to meet Mr. Baxter for lunch. For the life of me I can't remember his first name." Or questioned about some errand our spouse asked us to attend to, we answer, "Honey, I'm sorry. I forgot."

Since we do not generate new brain cells while slowly, steadily losing the ones we have, we may become forgetful, fail to process information speedily, or rely on old, not new, creative ways of doing things.

However, when memory loss is speeded by disease or accident, we face a more serious situation. Strangely some people become forgetful relatively early in life. Others retain good memories as long as they live.

Do realize that memory loss should not be mistaken for overall mental decline. Psychologists have discovered that, though memory may fail with age, judgment may improve. I note this particularly in the life of a loved one. She frequently forgets what day it is, whether or not she has taken her medication. She has difficulty remembering figures. Yet, she holds her own when we play *Probe* or *Scrabble*. She evaluates government and social issues with good rationale.

Most people can be taught to improve their memories. Conscious effort to remember days, schedules, whatever, is effective. What's wrong with suggesting to an aging parent that he jot down on a note pad things he specifically wants to remember?

You may ask a forgetful parent to mark on a calendar the times you telephone or visit. If complaints are voiced, you need only refer him to the notations on the calendar.

Erroneous Judgments

On one of his visits to Canada, the late Charles de Gaulle, then president of France, made several derogatory remarks about Canadian politics that caused severe repercussions. One European diplomat announced, "De Gaulle is getting old—he is nearly 77." Meanwhile in Montreal the assessment was far more harsh: "Senile!" people declared.

In reporting the incident, *Time* magazine[4] suggested that, though de Gaulle's remarks were upsetting, they in no way indicated he lacked mental astuteness. French physicians echoed this affirmation. As proof, they claimed: no mental lapses; memory as sharp as ever; speeches meticulously prepared and delivered from memory without notes.

Making derogatory remarks isn't the only factor that leads people to imply an elderly person is senile. Take Cora as an example. One night she awakened in her apartment, dizzy and nauseated. She summoned help. Temporarily confused, she found it difficult to reconstruct exactly what had happened. Family members shook their heads. "Senile. Mother's growing senile."

The doctor suspected a brain tumor and proceeded with related tests. His diagnosis negated, he enquired further. Eventually it was decided Cora suffered from anemia and a severe inner-ear malfunction. She recovered and though she is still a little forgetful, she hasn't lost her reasoning power. She is not senile.

A more shocking example of improper diagnosis involved a Minneapolis, Minnesota, man, Ludvig Hagen, 86 years old.

When his friend, Palmer Hanson, noticed that Hagen didn't seem to be home anymore, he decided to investigate.

A young woman answered the door. In response to Hanson's questions about Hagen's whereabouts, she said, "He is in a nursing home, but I don't know which one."

By chance Palmer Hanson read a notice stating that Hagen's belongings and his home were being sold since he was in a (named) nursing home.

Hanson promptly visited his friend. He was told not to mention to Hagen that his home was being sold, it might upset him. The staff suggested that Hagen wasn't clear mentally. They couldn't understand him. Hanson learned his friend often switched to the Norwegian language. When he spoke of his wife who had died four years previously, he expressed a desire to go home to be with her. Hanson was surprised that attendants didn't understand Hagen referred to a heavenly home.

When Hagen learned that someone claimed to have been appointed his conservator, he said he had asked for none. Moreover, he didn't want his home and possessions sold. He wanted to live in his home.

Eventually nursing home personnel compiled a discharge plan that could be used to assure Hagen's adequate care in his own home. Hanson, who at 79 still worked as a carpenter, told newspaper reporters that on one of his visits Hagen recited a religious poem for him. In parting he said, "Greet your wife from me."

"Does that sound as if he has lost his senses?" Hanson asked. "As far as I can see he's just as bright as he was a year ago. He's a little bit slower, but I can't see any difference as far as his mind is concerned."

I can't understand all the implications of the case. Apparently no charges were brought against the conservator or the nursing home because "they did what they thought was best at the time." Nevertheless, the incident frightens me. Another case of erroneous judgment because of temporary disorientation?

However, symptoms commonly considered evidence of senility—extreme disorientation, depression, memory loss, irritability, untidiness, insensitivity to others, oversensitivity to self, need to be watched.

Commonly linked to hardening of the arteries and to

brain disease, they may be triggered by unrecognized ailments, many of which can be controlled, sometimes cured. Even where the brain or blood vessels are affected, some persons can be helped.

Recent studies have linked mental disturbance with abnormal thyroid functioning, hyperthyroidism—overfunctioning, as well as hypothyroidism—underfunctioning, of the gland. Mental and emotional disturbances, it has been discovered, improve when thyroid problems are resolved.

At the University of Carolina, physicians studied a group of patients with thyroid disorders, including ten with hyperthyroidism. Seven of the ten had psychiatric problems. Four suffered memory loss and had difficulty concentrating. Anxiety, fatigue, and irritability were noted. Two patients complained they were depressed. Two suffered from delusions. Yet, in all instances, remarkable improvement occurred following corrective thyroid treatment.[5]

Anemia, an iron deficiency, emphysema, low blood sugar, drug toxicity, alcoholism, and diabetic comas also cause symptoms that suggest senile behavior. Properly treated and alleviated, behavior may be modified or reversed.

Take clogged arteries as another example. In some instances they are reamed to permit blood to flow more freely to the brain. A condition known as hydrocephalus (water on the brain) has also misled physicians. Remarkable results have been achieved through a ventricular shunt (bypass surgery) which corrects the situation and reverses senile behavior.

Reversible Brain Syndrome

Prominent psychologist Robert Butler says reversible brain syndromes "are characterized by fluctuating levels of awareness which may vary from mild confusion to stupor or active delirium. Hallucinations may be present, usually visual rather than the auditory type."[6] The patient may be disoriented, may mistake one person for another. Other intellectual functions can also be impaired. "Restlessness, unusual aggressiveness, and a dazed expression may be noted."

The syndrome may be caused by toxicity from medication,

surgical or emotional trauma, social isolation, a treatable mental illness, congestive heart failure, a diabetic coma, alcoholism, or dehydration.

Practitioners believe doctors may be ever so sincere in their diagnoses and opinions, nevertheless, you who have elderly parents should realize that researchers are constantly discovering new information and treatments and that reversals are possible.

Chronic Brain Disease

At this point we speak of established senility brought on by chronic brain disease. An irreversible condition, it places an enormous psychological burden on children who must watch a loving and caring parent lose his ability to care for himself, his ability to communicate sensibly and to think rationally.

When this happens, filial relationships are shattered. Elliot Weitzman, researcher and neurologist, says it is as if the afflicted person has lost his "humanness." [7]

Formerly thought to be caused chiefly by cerebral arteriosclerosis, it now appears that this is true in only a small fraction of cases. Most of the senile suffer from brain diseases that rob the afflicted of their intellectual capacities, judgment, and normal emotional and physical conduct.

Though doctors cannot pinpoint a specific cause, genes appear to play a promient role. And because the brain picture it presents is so different from other kinds of brain damage, children of an afflicted parent should insist that proper medical and psychiatric tests be administered to verify a diagnosis.

With chronic brain syndrome behavior patterns are drastically altered. Memory loss including both recent and past events occurs. Disorientation includes time, place, and people confusion.

I grieved when my mother grew so disoriented she didn't know where she lived or with whom. At different times I was her sister, her aunt, or her mother. Yet, I learned not to be ashamed of her behavior. She could as well have been suffering from cancer or some other disease.

At times I was able to laugh at her actions, as was the case one morning when she reached across the table, took my daughter's uneaten egg, and placed it on my husband's plate.

I have learned other people have had similar experiences. One evening a friend, whom I'll call Judy, visited her senile mother-in-law in a nursing home. Greatly disturbed, the woman attempted to console my friend because she "had evidence" her son, Judy's husband, was having an affair with another woman.

Judy scoffed at the idea. "Why, Tim always comes home right after work. And he never goes any place without me. Mother, you know he's honest as the day is long!"

"Judy, Judy," the woman countered, "how can you be so dumb?"

I chuckled when Judy told me this story. I was glad she, too, had learned to laugh at such episodes.

There will be times when you, too, will laugh. But, more frequently the tears will flow. Particularly when you recall the formerly alert, intelligent person your parent used to be. It's then you will turn to the Lord, again and again, as you seek His comfort and sustaining grace.

11.

Home Care
vs Institutional Care

"A Family Upside Down," the television program I mentioned previously, explored the whole gamut of filial relationships as they related to problems following an eldery parent's severe heart attack. Note the progress:

* A happy elderly couple, living in their own home, enjoy the love and companionship of each other and the good will of their adult children.

* A sudden heart attack frightens everyone.

* Following convalescence grandfather returns to his home despite differences of opinion.

* Later grandparents move to their adult son's home.

* Attendant problems—teenage son gives up his room; tension builds.

* A more serious episode requiring nursing-home care occurs. Increasing tension and unhappiness. Eventual change in grandfather's attitude.

* Final options.

The film opened with an episode showing the lead characters, played by Helen Hays and Fred Astaire, saying

95

goodbye to their adult son, his wife, and teenage grandson and returning to their own home.

Climbing the stairs to the rear entrance, grandfather experiences a heart attack.

With the speed of a whip cracking the air, life is turned upside down for *all* members of the family.

At this moment you may be enjoying the same "fair weather" relationship with your parents as this adult son did. Yet you realize the situation can change. You may even have anticipated future problems and wondered how well you will cope.

No doubt you'll prove you are a stronger person than you think. Whatever happens—an accident, a handicap, a devastating illness, or a parent's death, you will survive. It may be because you planned ahead. Or because of the support you will receive from your family, your friends and your church, or various social-service organizations. It may also be because experiences coping with one problem have given you insight and stamina to cope with the next.

This doesn't mean life will be easy. The elderly parent for whom you are responsible may not always be cooperative or flexible. You are now entering a new phase in your relationship with him. It is not the casual relationship you have enjoyed up to this time—friendly visits, telephone calls, shopping excursions, mini trips. . . . Instead it may involve drastic change when you invite your parent to live with you in your home or when you select an alternate care facility.

Dependency Changes

You'll be wise to plan ahead now, to decide what move a parent needs to make before he becomes too decrepit or seriously ill. Professionals advise: (1) Plan ahead and act while your parent is still functionally normal. (2) When you first recognize symptoms of deterioration and you believe your parent needs a more structured environment, aid him in making the decision himself while he is still competent to do so—then visit alternate facilities with him.

One social worker suggests children of elderly parents

learn to recognize the stages of dependency through which an aged person goes before he becomes totally dependent. The first involves minimal loss in ability to care for himself as physical strength begins to wane. The next represents an intermediary stage when an elderly parent is partially dependent on himself and partially dependent on others. The last, the final stage, is one of total dependency that requires a person to live in some type of health care facility because he cannot function unaided.

This last stage is evidenced when, even though your mother says, "I'll have you know, I can manage perfectly well," you discover she cannot monitor her medication, she gets lost in familiar surroundings, she loses all concept of time and place, or she leaves the gas stove burning. (My mother made a fire in a kitchen waste basket because, she said, "It was raining outside.")

You need not resolve the problems of stage three, however, before you resolve the ones manifested during stage one and two. This doesn't mean that you neglect making a long-range comprehensive plan of some kind. Such a plan relieves both your family and your parents of anxiety that might otherwise attend moving from one stage of caretaking to the next. Be flexible and prepared for change, but take care of today's concerns today; tomorrow's when tomorrow comes. "Sufficient unto the day is the evil thereof."[1]

Now let's go back to a period that precedes stage one. What are the options?

* You can encourage your parents to enter a life-time care complex.

   If your parents meet acceptance requirements, which usually means they possess sufficient funds and are totally independent, you can encourage them to enter a life-time care complex. When circumstances require them to give up their apartment and move to an intermediary care facility and finally to skilled nursing care in a nursing home, the transition can be made smoothly without undue trauma.

Life-time care is discussed more fully in Chapter 3.

* In stage one you can agree with your parent that he should stay in his own home. His strength, you will recall, is beginning to wane, yet he needs only minimal supervision.

Most old people wish to remain in a familiar setting as long as they can. Daphne Krause underscored this premise aptly when she said, "For the vast majority of people, their whole identity as a human being is where they have lived and what makes up their home. Their home is their way of life. It's their neighbors, their church, their grocery store. It's everything that makes them an individual."[2]

But being responsible for a parent in his own home can be a taxing assignment. You may need to arrange for someone to take over household cleaning; during brief periods of minor illness, someone to live in by the day.

You'll no doubt do the grocery shopping, accompany your parent to his doctor's appointment, take care of his laundry, at times arrange for him to visit friends.

When it becomes evident that he needs day-long supervision, you may try another option.

* You can invite your parent to live with your family in your home.

Whether you do so because it would be more economical or because of your compassion, advance planning is recommended.

A niche of his own is desirable if it can be arranged. Friends in Los Angeles built an apartment adjacent to, yet attached to, their home when "Momo," as they called grandmother, came to live with them. The arrangement worked very well. Momo was free to visit whenever she liked. She often did the baking for the family. Yet she could retreat and be by herself when she tired or when she just wanted to be alone.

In the television sequence I described earlier, no

such arrangement could be made. The teenage grandson reluctantly gave up his bedroom for the grandparents and moved into a den off the kitchen. He tried to be gracious, yet he resented the move—and the fact that both grandparents constantly asked, "Does that music have to be so loud?"

If your mother (and most often it is a widowed mother) can assist around the house, let her. Knowing she contributes will boost her ego and make her feel useful. You would only encourage dependency and boredom by doing yourself tasks she can do. Such action becomes sort of an exchange agreement. You do for her, and she does for you.

If a parent can help financially, accept this help graciously.

Apportion advice miserly.

Be prepared for friction. It isn't easy for two women accustomed to running their own homes always to be amiable. Yet frictions can be resolved, even if it takes a third person to negotiate tranquility.

Maintain whatever religious observances you are accustomed to. Remember it's through loving care personified that you prove your love for God.

* You can select a boarding or a foster home for your parents. These homes are operated for elderly people who do not need a great deal of nursing or medical care.

A woman, a ward of the state, whom I met when my husband and I lived in Minneapolis, Minnesota, has lived in two different "foster" homes in the last 15 years; in a loving Christian home for the past 10 years. Her caring "parents" treat her as a member of the family.

A member of our local church lives in a licensed boarding home, where she and three other elderly persons receive minimal health care.

You should be aware that there is a great deal of discussion among practitioners favoring the idea that adult children receive some type of remuneration for caring for aging parents in their own homes rather than having to place them elsewhere. Legislation to this effect may be forthcoming some time in the future.

All types of facilities should be investigated before any decision is made. Your parent should be consulted and in agreement with the placement. Talk it over with him. He has a "right," and its abuse, many people feel, ought to be punishable by law.

The issue, it appears, is not so much the place where an elderly parent lives but the circumstances of his or her daily life. If both you and your spouse are away from home earning a living or pursuing careers, it seems logical that your parents could be of great assistance to you in the home, despite the fact your mother may not be as tidy around the kitchen as she used to be. This doesn't mean that parents should become merely unpaid housemaids or maintenance men, or built-in baby-sitters. They ought to be allowed to indicate what roles they wish or are able to assume.

There are instances when adult children and their families are so busy with activities outside of the home that parents are neglected and in a sense are as much institutionalized as they would appear to be in some other care facility.

As likely as not, living together can cause friction, irritability, and conflict of life-styles. Finally the family realizes no good purpose is achieved by continuing the relationship. Then you may need to do as Dr. Arthur N. Schwartz advises, talk to your parent or parents. You might say, "We love to have you live with us, but it just doesn't seem to be working out. Perhaps we can decide together what would be a better arrangement."

Always there is danger that you will feel guilt, for people may say you are "putting a parent away. . . ." You need not feel guilty if it becomes impossible for you to care for a parent in your own home. We've already spoken of alternate arrangements. However, when physical ailments and disability intensifies dependence, you may have no choice but to consider an intermediary health-care facility.

Do realize there is a difference between this type of facility and a skilled nursing facility. An intermediary care facility (ICF) cares for persons who can't live independently because they aren't well enough. Though they don't need constant medical supervision and nursing attention, they may need assistance with bathing, dressing, and walking—as well as social and recreational attention.

* When your parent moves into the last stage, that of total dependency, a skilled nursing facility (SNF) may be required. Such a facility cares for persons who need constant supervision, skilled nursing care, and rehabilitation therapy.

Generally this care is reserved for persons with physical impairment. Many institutions, however, accept elderly persons who are seriously disoriented. A 3-day minimum hospitalization and a doctor's recommendation qualify a person for admission and for medicare assistance.

It's wise to investigate and visit several such facilities before making a final choice. Visit the dining room at mealtime; talk to residents. You can make an official visit when you speak to the administrator at a later date.

A book, *Choosing a Nursing Home,* by Jean Baron Nassau, suggests areas you should check before making a final decision:

—Accreditation, license, and certification for Medicare and Medicaid.

—Physical condition of the facility. Is it well located, cheerful, attractive, clean, and safe? Does it meet state fire codes?

—Nursing and medical care, social activities, physical therapy, and rehabilitation services.

—Food. Is it nutritious, carefully prepared in a clean kitchen and served in pleasant surroundings?

—Staff. Are members professionally trained, and is the number adequate?

—Hidden costs.

Do realize, however, that there are features far more important than clean floors and good food. You will want to learn if the facility genuinely cares for its residents. Does it do everything possible to make life worth living? Note how staff personnel speak to the elderly. How do they treat them?

"The most desirable facility," Dr. Arthur N. Schwartz claims, "literally saturates its week with a wide variety of activities to suit a wide variety of tastes and needs. It offers a veritable smorgasbord of opportunities for different residents to engage themselves in interesting and useful endeavors. There needs to be opportunity for recreation and entertainment . . . but also an opportunity to feel needed and useful."[4]

Having conscientiously investigated what is available to your parent, and having explored alternatives with him, you should be able to make a sensible and suitable choice. And be satisfied that you have done the best you could to serve your own interests and, more importantly, the interests of your parents.

Now your responsibility is to keep in touch, to continue demonstrating the love and concern so badly needed when one is isolated from family and friends.

12.
When It's Time
to Say Good-bye

Why is it that we read accounts of tragic accidents, manslaughter, death of long-time residents, and suicides unmoved, with scarcely any reaction other than a quick flip of the newspaper page?

Death Is Taboo

We are told such response is common since we live in a death-denying culture. This is true even in the church. We avoid talking about death. We minimize its impact through embalmings, cosmetics, and satin-lined coffins. Even the word *death* is taboo. We say someone has "passed on," "gone," or "departed."

As a child you, like other grownups, may have been "protected" by a shield of silence regarding death. You may not have been permitted to attend family funerals. When death was discussed or grief displayed, you were shunted off to play.

Even today, though death has become a very popular subject in the media, we tend to ignore it. Children, too, are affected. In many instances their concept of death comes chiefly from violent television programs.

I recall attending a funeral where, as isn't usually the

custom, several children were present. When one young lad stopped to view the deceased, he exclaimed, "Who shot him?"

In times past the terminally ill died in their own homes or in the homes of a loved one with members of the family around them. Not so today. According to Elisabeth Kubler-Ross, 80 percent of Americans die in institutions.[1]

No wonder, we, and the elderly in particular, have hang-ups about death. A new dimension has been added—fear of dying alone, separated from family and friends during our last hours of life. Many doctors say they would favor some plan by which people could die in their own homes. Yet this doesn't seem feasible. (How supportive could the medical profession be, timewise?) How desirable? (Are we prepared to accept the responsibility?)

Need for Concern

Whatever our feelings in this regard, concern for the elderly parent must include a consideration of death. And no matter what pressures you experience in your concern, none may be as difficult as learning that one's parent is terminally ill. Suddenly you contemplate what life will be without him. A link with the past will be broken.

If you have already tended to push aside thoughts about death, you may miss the blessing of closeness and rapport in the interim before a parent dies. He may hint that he wants to talk about his condition. He may say, "When I am gone. . . ." Or, "Well, you know I'm not going to be around much longer."

"Nonsense," you answer, "I may die long before you do." More appropriately you could say, "I'll miss you." Or, "Perhaps, but as long as you are around we're going to love and care for you."

After acknowledging possible imminence of death, your parent may feel free to discuss his will, the distribution of personal property, his desires regarding funeral and burial procedures.

Fortunate are the children whose parents have made such plans prior to becoming terminally ill. If not, they need to talk about them.

You'll feel more comfortable dealing with these matters if you understand whether a parent should be told about his illness, the stages through which he goes, how you can ease the trauma of dying, and what happens when he dies.

Telling the Truth

People who work closely with the dying feel strongly that frankness and honesty about a terminal illness should be the rule rather than the exception.

You may be convinced you are doing your mother a favor when you urge her doctor not to reveal the true facts about her illness. But is this kind? How can you explain weakness and increased pain? How will she react to evasions to questions she asks?

Though most doctors believe the terminally ill have the right to know the truth, many feel it is not necessary to go into great detail. Once your mother knows what's happening, she begins to prepare herself to ask questions, resolve past hurts, and make her peace with God if that is necessary.

Experience has taught that in most instances patients have already guessed the truth long before being told. They sense physicians are hurried and evasive. Nurses tend to routine duties and quickly leave. Family members appear ill at ease when they visit.

Stages of Dying

From hundreds of case histories, Dr. Elisabeth Kubler-Ross[3] has come to believe there are five emotional stages, of varying lengths of time, that patients pass through before they die. The first is shock that manifests itself in denial. "Not me. It can't be me," a patient says. This is true whether patients are told about their condition or come to this conclusion themselves.

Anger, the second stage, surfaces when the truth is acknowledged. Bitter, envious, a patient asks, "Why me? Why not her?" "I'm so young, much younger than he is." "It isn't fair."

During this stage patients take out their spite on everyone

and everything. Of all stages this may be the most difficult for you. But hang loose. Remain loving and caring in spite of abuse.

During the third stage, that of bargaining, patients make deals with God. "I'll do this or that, if You. . . ." A patient may wish to live until a great grandchild is born, until a son returns from overseas. As one deadline is met, another is proposed.

Step four involves depression. The burden becomes intolerable. Patients grow uncommunicative and withdraw. You who stand by should not minimize the patient's trauma. Many people have found that by reading Psalm 23 they have helped the one who grieves.

Then comes acceptance when patients acknowledge death is imminent. This is the time a patient may indicate concern about a hereafter. They may want to clear up past differences— either ask forgiveness for a wrong committed or extend forgiveness for something you have done. You can make it easy for them to do this by acknowledging wrong, real or imagined.

A well-known Catholic priest once said, "Don't cheat yourself out of the joy of reconciliation." He could as well have said, "Don't cheat yourself or your parents."

One day the son of a dying parishioner called my clergyman husband. "Pastor," he said, "My dad and I haven't spoken for 20 years. What can I do?"

"Be reconciled." my husband answered. "Take the first step."

He did this and his father died in peace.

Don't assume, however, that a dying person automatically turns to God. Yet, some do.

A man, for many years my denomination's president, had tried unsuccessfully for years to impress his business-executive brother with the need for a Savior. A few weeks before his brother's death, this man flew to his bedside. With tenderness and compassion, so typical of him, he was privileged to lead his brother to Christ.

Conversely, in some instances, a dying parent leads a son or daughter to Christ.

Do realize that a Christian goes through the same stages

that others do. Christians can deny, bargain with God, and grow depressed. Jesus knew sorrow. He wept over a city, after the death of a friend. Family members can comfort, accept, and pray that faith be sustained.

Emotional Needs

Specialists in the field have begun to speak about American negligence of the emotional needs of the terminally ill. At the very time they need us most, we withdraw.

A doctor friend claims that at no other time is it so necessary to demonstrate the "fruits of the Spirit": love, joy, peace, patience, gentleness, goodness, and faith. Death can be a very lonely experience. We need to pay attention. Medical personnel included.

In an article in *The Catholic Digest* (November 1975)[4] Sister M. Pamela Smith says nurses are usually so busy tending routine needs such as taking pulses, administering pills, keeping records, feeding, bathing, and changing beds that they fail to note a dying patient's anguish, depression, tears, or his desire to talk.

"People make jittery pop-in visits and jovially try to 'cheer up' the patient with flowers, light-hearted gossip, joke books, and candy," she says. Meanwhile a patient probably needs someone to linger, listen, and pray (audibly or silently).

Be sensitive to specific needs, however. A minister friend said that during a period of hospitalization when he wasn't expected to live, a host of clergymen friends visited him. "I was so desperately ill," he said, "one lengthy prayer after the other almost drove me crazy. One fellow, however, just came in, stood by my bedside and held my hand. That one gesture meant more to me than any audible prayer."

This does not rule out the need for devotional support, however. A terminally ill parent may welcome a devotional time when you read a favorite portion of Scripture, a meaningful poem or article. Then don't hesitate to pray with and for your parent.

It's important, too, to keep your parent's pastor informed of any illness and hospitalization. Clergymen are often accused

107

of negligence and indifference when actually they have not been informed of the situation.

Realize, also, that hospital chaplains stand ready to comfort and cheer. Alert them to your parent's physical and spiritual needs, to voiced fears and failures. Often dying persons find it easier to confide in a concerned outsider than they do in members of their own family.

Check with hospital personnel to learn when would be the best time for your parent to receive Communion, either from the chaplain or from the pastor. If possible, participate with your parent in this bedside sacrament. Your presence will mean more than you realize.

Speaking of her experiences in nursing homes, Sister Smith,[5] indicated she had learned to be perceptive about patient's needs: when to suggest a game of Parcheesi; when to bring a rose; when to read; when to pray; when to sit on a bed in silence holding a hand; and when to kiss a patient goodnight.

A speaker at a gerontology conference described his last visit to the hospital where his grandfather lay dying.

Like the patriarchs of old, his grandfather called his children and his grandchildren to his bedside. He asked them to hold hands as he prayed for them. Then he blessed them, petitioning God and His Holy Spirit to guide them and to sustain them in their faith.

What Happens When a Person Dies

Until recently a person's last heartbeat and last breath marked the termination of life. Today, because of advanced technology, both heart and lungs can be resuscitated after having stopped. Doctors can keep a patient's body alive, at least with the heartbeat, when there is no brain function at all. Thus doctors tend to consider termination of life when the "brain dies," which means the cells have been deprived of oxygen to such an extent that they die.

Because life can be sustained when a person becomes no more than a vegetable, many individuals indicate to others that they want to die with dignity. They sign what is known as a "living will." Though not legally binding, it is addressed "To my family, my physician, my clergyman. To any medical facility in whose care I happen to be. To any individual who may become responsible for my health, welfare, or affairs." The document states:

> If the situation should arise in which there is no reasonable expectation of my recovery from physical or mental disability, I request that I be allowed to die and not be kept alive by artificial means or 'heroic measure.' I do not fear death itself as much as the indignities of deterioration, dependence, and hopeless pain. I, therefore, ask that medication be mercifully administered to me to alleviate suffering, even though this may hasten my death.

In considering what it means to die, take with a grain of apprehension the clamor about the book *Life After Life*.[6] Christians agree that death does not terminate life. However, the type of life we experience after this life depends on the preparation we have made for it beforehand. "For if we have been planted together in the likeness of His death, we shall be also in the likeness of His resurrection." [7]

If and when you read Dr. Raymond Moody's book, ask: Where does Christ enter the picture? Is He the light at the end of the dark tunnel in all the case histories? Could some of the experiences have been the result of dreams or drug hallucinations? Could the emphasis of "all light and glory" deceive persons unprepared to meet their Creator?

Though many Christians have described "welcoming visions" at the end of this life, death is not always so kind. Death can be extremely traumatic, and you don't need to feel guilty if a Christian parent doesn't leave this life in a "blaze of glory."

Funerals

When you consult a mortician and a clergyman about your parent's funeral service, try to carry out his wishes concerning cremation, burial, pre-service viewal, private graveside ceremony. Honor his choice of speakers, musicians, and music.

Increasingly people opt not to view the body, yet

psychologists claim that for some individuals this practice is therapeutic. It helps verify the fact a loved one has actually died.

Coping with Grief

According to statistics, most likely one of your parents will survive the other. Let's say your father dies first. No matter how you may have imagined you'd feel, you aren't prepared for such a mixture of emotions. You'll feel lonely and bereft. You may feel angry that all that your father represented is gone. You may feel guilty. You may wish you had taken his advice about not going into business for yourself, that you missed so many opportunities for companionship. You may feel sad, so sad you seek a place where you can cry unashamedly. This is natural.

Yet, while you mourn your father, you need to understand the needs and feelings of your mother, who also grieves. Grieving is normal, not to grieve is abnormal—unless a spouse admits, as one woman did at a gerontology workshop, "I was happy and relieved when my husband passed away."

Following the funeral of your father, your grief-stricken mother may become restless and engage in activities in which your father was interested.

Or, she may refuse to accept his death, insist on keeping workroom or office intact, and refuse to dispose of his clothing.

You and your family can help your mother work through her grief by talking about your father. Recall the good times, as well as the bad, that you had together.

Make sure your support continues. Too often we smother those who grieve with love and attention immediately and forget them after the funeral. Your mother needs sustained attention—but not overindulgence. Be especially attentive on birthdays, anniversaries, especially on the anniversary of your father's death.

If your mother expresses guilt feelings voiced by, "If only I had done so and so," assure her that "so and so" may not have made the slightest difference.

Evaluation

No matter what you do or have done for your elderly parents, you may never feel that you did enough. Nevertheless, if you believe you have done your best, you've done what is expected of you. And who could ask for more?

Where to Go for Help

CONSUMER INFORMATION

Protection for the Elderly. (Consumer Bulletin No. 9). Free from Federal Trade Commission, 6th and Pennsylvania Ave. N. W., Washington, D.C. 20508.

Consumer Guide for Older People. Administration on Aging, Washington, D.C. 20201. Publication SRS 72-20801. Free.

How to Pay Less for Prescription Drugs, How to Find a Doctor for Yourself, From *Consumer Reports* (Reprint Department), Consumers Union, Orangeburg, N.Y., 10962.

CRIME PREVENTION

Preventing Crime Through Education: How to Spot a Con Artist. NRTA/AARP, 1901 K Street N. W., Washington, D.C. Free.

EDUCATION

Write to nearby colleges and universities for information on their participation in "lifetime learning" programs.

HEALTH

Health Aspects of Aging. American Medical Association, 535 North Dearborn St., Chicago, Illinois, 60610. 20¢.

Your Guide to Good Health. Metropolitan Life Insurance Co., One Madison Ave., New York, N.Y. 10010.

Public Affairs Pamphlets. Catalog of inexpensive booklets on social and economic problems, family life, physical and mental health. Public Affairs Inc., 381 Park Ave. S., New York, N.Y., 10016.

Medicare/Medicaid Benefits, Home Health Care. Department of Health, Education and Welfare, Washington, D.C. 20201.

LEGAL AND FINANCIAL MANAGEMENT

You, the Law and Retirement (OHD/AoA 73-20800). Superintendent of Documents, U.S. Government Printing Office, Washington, D.C. 20402. 45¢.

Dollars and Sense After Sixty, by Louis L. Himber. Division on Aging, Federation of Protestant Welfare Agencies, 281 Park Avenue S., New York, N.Y. 10010. Free.

NURSING HOMES

Nursing Home Care. Published by the Social and Rehabilitation Service, U.S. Department of Health, Education, and Welfare, Washington, D.C. 20201.

Directory of Nursing Homes. Membership Service Dept. AAHA, 1050 17th St., N. W., Washington, D.C., 20036. $20. Can be examined in public libraries.

NUTRITION

The U.S. Department of Agriculture (USDA) publishes a series of pamphlets on good nutrition. Order from USDA. Free. Or for a small cost from the U.S. Government Printing Office, Washington, D.C., 20402.

Food Guide for Older Folks. (USDA) Home and Garden Bulletin No. 17. (U.S. Government Printing Office, No. 1011-03321. 40¢).

Cooking for Two, USDA Program Aid No. 1043. (U.S. Government Printing Office No. 0100-03327. $1.25).

Food for Fitness, USDA No. 424. (U.S. Government Printing Office No. 0100-02882. 15¢).

Meal Planning for the Golden Years. General Mills, Inc.

Nutrition Service Department 5, 9200 Wayzata Blvd., Minneapolis, Minnesota, 55440.

Cooking for One in the Senior Years. Cooperative Extension, N.Y. State College of Human Ecology, Cornell University, Ithaca, New York 14953. 20¢.

PHYSICAL FITNESS

The Fitness Challenge in the Later Years: An Exercise Program for Older Americans. U.S. Department of Health, Education, and Welfare, Administration on Aging, Washington, D.C., 200201.

Aiming for Dynamic Fitness. Action for Independent Maturity, 1909 K. Street N. W., Washington, D.C. 20006.

RETIREMENT

After 65: Resources for Self-Reliance, by Theodore Irwin. Public Affairs Pamphlet No. 501, Public Affairs Committee, Inc., 381 Park Avenue S., New York, N.Y. 10016.

Getting Ready to Retire, by Kathryn Close. Public Affairs Pamphlet No. 182. Same Address.

Begin Now to Enjoy Tomorrow. Mutual Benefit Life, Box 520, Newark, N.J. 07101.

Planning for Retirement. Consumer and Community Services, Institute of Life Insurance, 277 Park Ave., New York, N.Y. 10017.

Write also to the Publication Office, Andrus Gerontology Center, University of California, University Park, Los Angeles, California, 90007, for its *pamphlet series.* 50¢ each.

SAFETY

Handle Yourself with Care. Administration on Aging, Washington, D.C., 20201. Free.

TRAVEL

NRTA/AARP Travel Service, 555 Madison Ave., New York, N.Y. 10022.

Tour Department, National Council of Senior Citizens, Inc., 1511 K. Street N. W., Washington D.C. 20005.

VOLUNTEER PROGRAMS

ACTION, the coordinating agency for the federal government's volunteer programs includes Retired Senior Volunteer Programs (RSVP), which provides grants for the development and operation of programs for persons 60 years of age and over; the Foster Grandparent Program, the Service Corps of Retired Executives (SCORE); the Peace Corps, Volunteers in Service to America (VISTA), and the Senior Companion Program.

Write: ACTION, Washington, D.C. 20525, or call ACTION'S toll-free telephone number 800-424-8580.

Green Thumb offers part-time jobs in rural areas. Write the Farmers Union, 1012 Fourteenth St. N. W., Washington, D.C. 2004.

STATE OFFICES ON THE AGING

Alabama: Commission on Aging, 740 Madison Ave., Montgomery 36104, (205) 832-6640

Alaska: Office on Aging, Department of Health and Social Services, Pouch H, Juneau 99811, (907) 586-6153

Arizona: Bureau on Aging, Department of Economic Security, 543 East McDowell, Room 217, Phoenix 85004, (602) 271-4446

Arkansas: Office on Aging and Adult Services, Department of Social and Rehabilitation Services, 7 and Gaines; P.O. Box 2179, Little Rock 72202, (501) 371-2441

California: Office on Aging, Health and Welfare Agency, 455 Capitol Mall, Suite 500, Sacramento 95814, (916) 322-3887

Colorado: Division of Services for the Aging, Department of Social Services, 1575 Sherman St., Denver 80203, (303) 892-2651/2586

Connecticut: Department on Aging, 90 Washington St., Room 312, Hartford 06115, (203) 566-2480

Delaware: Division on Aging, Department of Health and

Social Services, 2407 Lancaster Ave., Wilmington 19805, (302) 571-3481/3482

District of Columbia: Division of Services to the Aged, Department of Human Resources, 1329 E. St. N. W., Washington, D.C. 20004, (202) 638-2406

Florida: Division on Aging, Department of Health and Rehabilitation Services, 1323 Winewood Blvd., Tallahassee 32301, (904) 488-4797

Georgia: Office of Aging, Department of Human Resources, 47 Trinity Avenue, Atlanta 30334, (404) 894-5333

Hawaii: Commission on Aging, 1149 Bethel St., Room 311, Honolulu 96813, (808) 548-2593

Idaho: Idaho Office on Aging, Statehouse, Boise 83720, (208) 964-3833

Illinois: Department on Aging, 2401 West Jefferson St., Springfield 62762, (217) 525-5773

Indiana: Indiana Commission on Aging and Aged, Graphic Arts Building, 215 North Senate Ave., Indianapolis 46202, (317) 633-5948

Iowa: Commission on the Aging, 415 West 10th St., Jewett Building, Des Moines 50319, (515) 281-5182

Kansas: Department of Social and Rehabilitation Services, Services for the Aging Section, State Office Building, Topeka 66612, (913) 296-3465

Kentucky: Aging Program Unit, Department of Human Resources, 403 Wapping St., Frankfort 40601, (502) 564-6930

Louisiana: Bureau of Aging Services, Division of Human Resources, P.O. Box 44282, Capitol Station, Baton Rouge 70804, (504) 389-2171/6518

Maine: Office of Maine's Elderly, Community Services Unit, Augusta 04330, (207) 622-6171

Maryland: Office on Aging, State Office Building, 301 East Preston St., Baltimore 21201, (301) 383-5064/2100

Massachusetts: Department of Elderly Affairs, 120 Boylston St.,

Boston 02116, (617) 727-7751/7752

Michigan: Offices of Service to the Aging, 3500 North Logan St., Lansing 48913, (517) 373-5230

Minnesota: Governor's Citizens Council on Aging, Suite 204, Metro Square Building, 7 and Robert St., St. Paul 55101, (612) 296-2770

Mississippi: Council on Aging, P.O. Box 5136, Fondren Station, 510 George St., Jackson 39216, (601) 354-6590

Missouri: Office of Aging, Department of Social Services, Broadway State Office Building, P.O. Box 570, Jefferson City 65101, (314) 751-2075

Montana: Aging Services Bureau, Department of Social and Rehabilitation Service, P.O. Box 1723, Helena 59601, (406) 499-3124

Nebraska: Commission on Aging, State House Station 94784, 300 South 17th St., Lincoln 68509, (402) 471-2307

Nevada: Division of Aging, Dept. of Human Resources, 201 S. Fall St., Room 300, Nye Building, Carson City 89701, (702) 885-4210

New Hampshire: Council on Aging, P.O. Box 786, 14 Depot St., Concord 03301, (603) 271-2751

New Jersey: Division on Aging, Department of Community Affairs, P.O. Box 2768, 363 West State St., Trenton 08625, (609) 292-3765

New Mexico: Commission on Aging, 408 Galisteo Villagra Building, Santa Fe 87503, (505) 827-5258

New York: Office for the Aging, New York State Executive Dept., 855 Central Ave., Albany 12206, (518) 457-7321 New York State Office of the Aging, 2 World Trade Center, Room 5036, New York 10047, (212) 488-6405

North Carolina: Governor's Coordinating Council on Aging, Administration Building, 213 Hillsborough St., Raleigh 27603, (919) 829-3983

North Dakota: Aging Services, Social Services Board of North Dakota, State Capitol Building, Bismark 58505 (701) 224-2577

Ohio: Commission on Aging, 35 North High St., Columbus 43215, (614) 466-5500/5501

Oklahoma: Special Unit on Aging, Social and Rehabilitation Services, Box 25352, Capitol Station, Oklahoma City 73125, (405) 521-2281

Oregon: Program on Aging, Human Resources Dept., 772 Commercial St., S. E., Salem 97310, (503) 378-4728

Pennsylvania: Office for the Aging, Department of Public Welfare, Capitol Associates Building, 7 and Forster St., Harrisburg 17120, (717) 787-5300

Puerto Rico: Gericulture Commission, Dept. of Social Services, P.O. Box 11697, Santurce 00908, (809) 722-2429

Rhode Island: Division on Aging, Dept. of Community Affairs, 150 Washington, Providence 02903, (401) 277-2858

South Carolina: Commission on Aging, 915 Main St., Columbia 29201, (803) 758-2576

South Dakota: Office on Aging, Dept. of Social Services, St. Charles Hotel, Pierre 57501, (605) 224-3656

Tennessee: Commission on Aging, Room 102 S and P Building, 306 Gay St., Nashville 37201, (615) 741-2056

Texas: Governor's Commission on Aging, 8th Floor Southwest Tower, 211 East 7th St., P.O. Box 12786, Capitol Station, Austin 78711, (512) 475-2717

Utah: Division on Aging, Department of Social Services, 345 South 6th St., Salt Lake City 84102, (801) 328-5422

Vermont: Office on Aging, Agency for Human Services, 81 River Street (Heritage 1), Montpelier 05602, (802) 770-7894

Virginia: Office on Aging, 830 East Main Street, Suite 950, Richmond 23219, (804) 770-7894

Virgin Islands: Commission on Aging, P.O. Box 539, Charlotte Amalie, St. Thomas 00801, (809) 774-5884

Washington: Office on Aging, Department of Social and Health Services, P.O. Box 1788, M.S. 45-2, Olympia 98504, (206) 753-2502

West Virginia: Commission on Aging, State Capitol,

Charleston 25305, (304) 348-3317

Wisconsin: Division on Aging, Department of Health and Social Services, 1 East Wilson St., Room 686, Madison 53702, (608) 266-2536

Wyoming: Aging Services, Department of Health and Social Services, New State Office Building West, Room 288, Cheyenne 82002, (307) 777-7561

Notes

Chapter 1

1. S. Richard, R. Livson, and P.G. Peterson, *Aging and Personality* (New York: John Wiley and Sons, 1962).
2. Vern L. Bengtson, *The Social Psychology of Aging* (Indianapolis, New York: Bobbs Merrill Co., 1973), p. 34.
3. Margaret J. Anderson, *Looking Ahead—The Realities of Aging: Face Them with Faith* (Saint Louis, Missouri: Concordia Publishing House, 1978).

Chapter 2

1. Barbara Corcoran, "The Man of Your Choice," *Woman's Day*, November 1966, p. 47.
2. Robert Butler, *Why Survive? Being Old in America* (New York: Harper and Row, 1975).

Chapter 3

1. Barbara Silverstone and Helen Kandel Hyman, *You and Your Aging Parents* (New York: Pantheon Books, 1975), p. 30.

Chapter 4

1. Silverstone and Hyman, p. 9.

Chapter 5

1. Howard Whitman, "Deferred Payments," *The Later Life* (New York: Prentis Hall, Inc., 1961).
2. National Broadcasting Company, produced by Ross Hunter and Jacques Mates, sponored by Xerox Corporation, *A Family Upside Down*, televised April 9, 1978.
3. Anonymous, "I Had to Ask My Mother to Move Out of My House," *Good Housekeeping Magazine*, November 1977, p. 38.

Chapter 6

1. *The Oregonian*, February 25, 1978.
2. *Modern Maturity*, August/September, 1977.
3. *Modern Maturity*, August/September, 1978. Address: 215 Long Beach Blvd., Long Beach, CA 90801.

Chapter 8

1. Lawrence Galton, *Don't Give Up on an Aging Parent* (New York: Crown Publishing, Inc., 1975), p. 21.
2. Ibid. pp. 16, 17.
3. Margaret J. Anderson, *Looking Ahead—The Realities of Aging: Face Them with Faith* (Saint Louis, Missouri: Concordia Publishing House, 1978).
4. Robert Mendelsohn, M.D., "People's Doctor," Syndicated Column, June 7, 1978.
5. Daniel C. Brown, *Medical Tribune;* Vol. 19, No. 4, p. 1.
6. *Report to International Cardiovascular Society*, Rochester, New York, Meeting of Otology, Rhinology, and Laryngology; Vol. 867, p. 357.
7. *Annals of Otology, Rhinology, ad Laryngology*, Vol. 86, p. 357.

Chapter 9

1. Amanda A. Beck, *Michigan Aging Citizens: Characteristics, Opinions, and Service Utilizations* (Ann Arbor, Michigan:

University of Michigan—Wayne University, 1975).

2. Shirley Margolius, *Health Foods: Facts and Fakes* (New York: Walker and Company, 1973, reprinted in 1975), Public Affairs Pamphlet No. 499, p. 5.

3. Jean Mayer, "Pills, Promises, and Potions," *Family Health,* June 1977.

4. Virginia and Norman Rohrer, *How to Eat Right and Feel Great* (Wheaton, Illinois: Tyndale House Publishers), 1977.

5. Lawrence Galton, *Don't Give Up on an Aging Parent* (New York: Crown Publishers, 1975), pp. 161-165.

Chapter 10

1. Barbara Silverstone and Helen Kandel Hyman, *You and Your Aging Parents* (New York: Pantheon Books, 1975), p. 67.

2. Tim LaHaye, *How to Win over Depression* (Grand Rapids: Zondervan Publishing House, 1974), p. 49-58.

3. *The Bible,* The Book of Job.

4. *Time,* August 4, 1967, p. 45.

5. P.C. Whybrow, "Mental Changes Accompanying Thyroid Gland Disfunction," *Archives of General Psychology,* Vol. 20, p. 48.

6. Robert Butler, *Why Survive? Being Old in America* (New York: Harper and Row, 1975), pp. 175-176.

7. *Geriatric Focus,* June 1, 1968.

Chapter 11

1. *The Bible,* Matthew 6:34.

2. Daphne Krause, executive director, Minneapolis Age and Opportunity Center, quoted in *Congressional Record,* September 9, 1975, p. S15522.

3. Jean Baron Nassau, *Choosing a Nursing Home* (New York: Funk and Wagnalls, 1975).

4. Arthur N. Schwartz, *Survival Handbook for Children of Aging Parents* (Chicago: Follett Publishing Co., 1977), pp. 127-128.

Chapter 12

1. Elisabeth Kubler-Ross, *On Death and Dying* (New York: MacMillan Publishing Co., 1969).

2. Ibid.

3. Ibid.

4. Sister M. Pamela Smith, "Death, Be Not Lonely," condensed from *Sisters Today* (Collegeville, Minnesota: St. John's Abbey), June/July 1975.

5. Ibid.

6. Raymond A. Moody, Jr., *Life After Life* (Mockingbird Books, 1975).

7. *The Bible,* Romans 6:5

Bibliography

Anderson, Margaret A. *Looking Ahead—The Realities of Aging: Face Them with Faith.* Saint Louis: Concordia Publishing House, 1978.

Atchley, Robert. *The Social Forces in Later Life.* Belmont, California: Wadsworth Publishing Co., 1972.

Bengston, Vern L. *The Social Psychology of Aging.* Indianapolis; New York: Bobbs Merrill Co., Inc., 1973.

Bengston, Vern L. "You, Your Children, and Their Children," a lecture series edited by Barbara O'Brien. Los Angeles: The University of Southern California Press, 1978.

Butler, Robert N. *Why Survive? Being Old in America.* New York: Harper and Row Publishers, Inc., 1975.

Butler, R.N., and M. Lewis. *Aging and Mental Health* (second edition). Saint Louis, Missouri: J. Mosby and Co., 1977.

Davis, Richard H. *Aging: Today's Research and You,* edited by Beatrice O'Brien. Los Angeles: University of Southern California Press, 1978.

Galton, Lawrence, *Don't Give Up on an Aging Parent.* New York: Crown Publishers, 1978.

Kubler-Ross, Elisabeth, *On Death and Dying.* New York: MacMillan Co., 1969.

LaHaye, Tim, *How to Win over Depression*. Grand Rapids: Zondervan Publishing House, 1971.

Otten, Jean, and Florence Shelley. *When Your Parents Grow Old*. New York: Thomas G. Crowell Co., Inc., 1976, 1977.

Percy, Charles H. *Growing Old in the Country of the Young*. New York: McGraw-Hill Book Co., 1974.

Robinowitz, Dorothy, and Yedda Nielson. *Home Life*. New York: The MacMillan Co., 1971.

Rohrer, Virginia and Norman. *How to Eat Right and Feel Great*. Wheaton, Illinois: Tyndale House Publishers, 1977.

Silverstone, Barbara, and Helen Kandel. *You and Your Aging Parents,* New York: Pantheon Books; Toronto: Random House, 1976.

Schwartz, Arthur N. *Survival Handbook for Children of Aging Parents*. Chicago: Follett Publishing Co., 1977.

Weg, Ruth B. *Nutrition and the Later Years*. Los Angeles: University of Southern California Press, 1978.